NCE Essential Test Tips DVD
from Trivium Test Prep!

Dear Customer,

Thank you for purchasing from Trivium Test Prep! We're honored to help you prepare for your NCE.

To show our appreciation, we're offering a **FREE *NCE Essential Test Tips* DVD by Trivium Test Prep**. Our DVD includes 35 test preparation strategies that will make you successful on the NCE. All we ask is that you email us your feedback and describe your experience with our product. Amazing, awful, or just so-so: we want to hear what you have to say!

To receive your **FREE *NCE Essential Test Tips* DVD**, please email us at 5star@triviumtestprep.com. Include "Free 5 Star" in the subject line and the following information in your email:

1. The title of the product you purchased.

2. Your rating from 1 – 5 (with 5 being the best).

3. Your feedback about the product, including how our materials helped you meet your goals and ways in which we can improve our products.

4. Your full name and shipping address so we can send your FREE *NCE Essential Test Tips* DVD.

If you have any questions or concerns please feel free to contact us directly at 5star@triviumtestprep.com.

Thank you!

IELTS Academic Study Guide 2021-2022:

Comprehensive Review with Audio and Practice Questions for the International English Language Testing System Exam

Elissa Simon

TABLE OF CONTENTS

The comprehension of different psychological theories helps a counselor to understand human thoughts, emotions and behaviors. Learning about the theories and theorists also helps a student to learn different therapeutic techniques, application of theories, and also ethical codes. There are theories that address behavior, development, cognition, career and more. This overview will help you to understand the various theories and theorists as well as application of theories.

BEHAVIOR THEORY

Behavior theory springs from the idea that all behaviors are learned and acquired through a process known as conditioning. This theory is most often associated with two psychologists: John B. Watson and B.F. Skinner. Behavior therapy concentrates on the observable behaviors of a person or group, and dismisses internal mental states. Other key components of Behavior Theory are conditioning, reinforcement and punishment. Behavioral theories dominated psychology during the early half of the twentieth century, and behavioral techniques are still widely used in therapeutic settings to help clients learn new skills and behaviors.

John B. Watson, a prominent psychologist who espoused behavior theory, stated this in his 1930 book *Behaviorism*:

"Give me a dozen healthy infants, well-formed, and my own specified world to bring them up in and I'll guarantee to take any one at random and train him to become any type of specialist I might select -- doctor, lawyer, artist, merchant-chief and, yes, even beggar-man and thief, regardless of his talents, penchants, tendencies, abilities, vocations, and race of his ancestors."

According to Watson, all human behavior can be studied in a systematic, observable way. Behavioral theory does not take into count the concepts of emotion or even the unconscious or subconscious, as these states are subjective and not objective. Behaviorists believe that all behavior can be trained. There are two forms of training or conditioning:

- *Classical Conditioning*: A process in which a subject comes to respond to a stimulus that was previously considered neutral. Continued exposure to this stimulus will elicit a desired response. For example: Maureen is in first grade and she is demonstrating difficulty playing well with her peers. Her teacher puts her on a sticker program, where she earns a sticker each day she plays well with the other students and does not earn a sticker when she has a conflict. At the end of the week, she can earn a prize if she has four out of five stickers. Maureen would previously have viewed a sticker as

7

a neutral stimulus, but she now considers it a reward. The intention is to use the stickers as a short-term reward and the prize as a long-term reward. These rewards are meant to change the negative behavior (difficulty with peers) to a positive behavior (playing well with peers).

- *Operant conditioning.* A process in which a subject engages in the correct behavior though the use of both rewards and punishments for a response. The subject learns to associate the behavior with the outcome. For example: Maureen is in first grade and she is demonstrating difficulty playing well with her peers. Her teacher puts her on a sticker program, where she earns a sticker each day she plays well with the other students and she receives a time out when she has a conflict. Maureen would learn to associate positive behavior with positive outcome (sticker) and negative behavior with punishment (time out).

Watson created a behavioral psychology theory based on the idea that human beings respond to their environment; external stimuli, not internal stimuli. He believed that all human beings could change their behavior through classical or operant conditioning.

B.F. Skinner, another famous behavioral theorist, said:

"The consequences of behavior determine the probability that the behavior will occur again."

B.F. Skinner, another famous behavioral theorist, developed the following schedules of reinforcement:

- *Continuous reinforcement*: This type of schedule reinforces the subject every time the desired behavior occurs. It is most commonly used during initial stages of learning to create the connection between the behavior and the response.

- *Partial reinforcement*: This type of schedule reinforces the subject only some of the times that the desired behavior occurs. There are four types of partial reinforcement:
  - *Fixed ratio*: a response reinforced after a predetermined number of responses. This schedule produces a high, steady rate of responses. An example of a fixed-ratio schedule would be giving a subject a piece of candy after they answer five questions correctly.
  - *Variable ratio*: a response reinforced after an unpredictable number of responses. This schedule creates a high steady rate of responding. An example is a slot machine hitting a win or a jackpot.

- *Fixed interval:* a response rewarded after a specified amount of time. An example is a subject being rewarded after two minutes of activity and then after each two minutes of activity.
- *Variable interval:* a response rewarded after an unpredictable amount of time has passed. An example would be rewarding a subject after one minute of activity, three minutes of activity, six minutes of activity and so on.

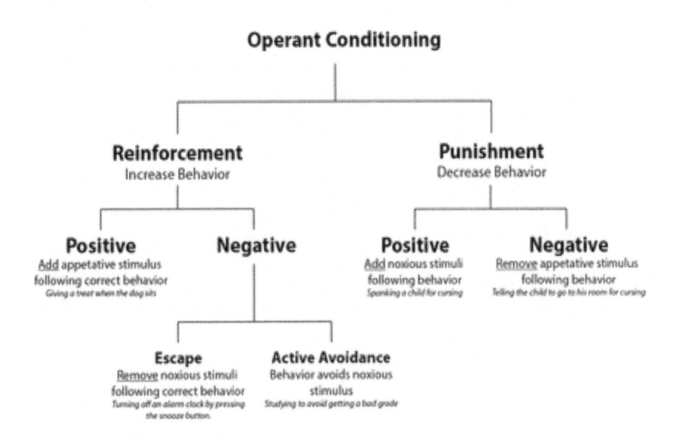

Postive presence of a stimulus

Negative absense of a stimulus

Reinforcement increases behavior

Punishment decreases behavior

Escape removes a stimulus

Avoidance prevents a stimulus

Behavior therapists also use approximation and shaping to elicit and reinforce correct responses. If a behavior never occurs, it is not in the person's repertoire. Shaping is a way of adding behaviors to a person's repertoire. Shaping is used when the target behavior does not yet exist. In shaping, what is reinforced is an approximation of the target behavior.

Approximation means any behavior that resembles the desired behavior or takes the person closer to the desired behavior. Successive approximations are steps toward the target behavior, the behavior you want to shape.

The general rule is that you are reinforcing any behavior that is a closer approximation of the target behavior than the behavior you reinforced last. If a new approximation does not occur, you reinforce the last approximation again. If an approximation is repeated and reinforced three times, you can withhold reinforcement the next time that behavior appears. If no new approximation appears, you have to drop back to a previously reinforced behavior. Sometimes you will get good progress for a while, only to have the child emit a behavior that was reinforced several steps before. You may then have to reinforce that old behavior and shape through the sequence again.

Edward Thorndike, another famous behavioral theorist, said:

"Human beings are accustomed to think of intellect as the power of having and controlling ideas, and of the ability to learn as synonymous with the ability to have ideas. But learning by having ideas is really one of the rare and isolated events in nature."

Thorndike is best-known for his theory called the law of effect. His theory states that responses that are immediately positively reinforced are more likely to occur again in the future. In addition, responses that are immediately negatively reinforced are less likely to occur again in the future.

COGNITIVE THEORY

Cognitive theories of psychology are focused on a person's thought processes, such as motivation, problem solving, decision-making, thinking, and attention.

Aaron Beck, a famous cognitive theorist, wrote:

"Sometimes the hardest part isn't letting go, but rather learning to start over."

Beck is most noted for his work in cognitive theory. He founded the Beck Institute for Cognitive Therapy, believing that people have "automatic thoughts" which are spontaneous negative cognitive distortions. Beck believed that there were three categories of cognitive distortions: negative thoughts about self, negative thoughts about the world and negative thoughts about the future. He believed that these negative thoughts affected a person's behavior. Regardless of the disorder a person is experiencing, Beck believed that if the negative thoughts could be identified, they could be evaluated and replaced. This would then change a person's response or behavior.

Beck believed that people can have one or many of the following cognitive distortions:

- **Filtering:** The negative details of a situation are magnified and all positive details of the situation are deleted. The person then dwells on the negative of the situation.

- **Polarized Thinking:** Situations, people or places are either "all or nothing. For example, a person either loves or hates others, or perceives situations as "the best ever" or "the worst ever."

- **Overgeneralization:** Based on one experience or little information, a person draws a conclusion. For example if a person got into a car accident at a store parking lot, they might come to view the store as dangerous and refuse to return.

- **Catastrophizing:** A person expects the worst, even when there is evidence to suggest otherwise. For example, a person might not apply for a job, thinking they wouldn't get it anyway – so why bother?

- **Personalization:** The belief that every response is directed at the person and that they are the cause of external events or feelings. For example, a victim may blame themselves for leaving their house for work late, perceiving that their own lateness was the cause of the car accident.

- **Control Fallacies:** A person sees himself or herself as a victim and believes that the external world has an inordinate amount of control over him or her. For example, someone might say, "I wouldn't have forgotten my work assignment if my boss didn't give me so much work." There are also internal control fallacies where a person views themselves as responsible. In this example, someone might say, "My boss is mad at me because he didn't greet me today." There are also fallacies of control, which is a belief that life in general is not fair.

- **Blaming:** A person blames others for their situation, such as attributing the cause of negative behaviors to others' actions.

- **Shoulds:** A belief in the "should and should nots". For example, someone might think, "I should eat healthier. I should not eat all these chips. If I was stronger, I wouldn't be so fat."

- **Emotional Reasoning:** A belief that emotions are thoughts, or the thought that because one thinks or feels something, it must be true. For example, a thought might be, "I don't feel like working today, so I must be depressed."

- **Always Being Right:** A person's need to go to all lengths to prove themselves right, even when evidence suggests otherwise.

Mindfulness cognitive therapy is mostly used for medical and emotional issues. Mindfulness helps a person to identify negative incoming thoughts or physical responses. Being aware of the negative helps the person to be aware or mindful without becoming attached or reacting. Mindfulness allows the person to be aware and then cope with the situation using multiple techniques. An example is someone who has been experiencing depression. When a person feels overwhelmed and has no motivation, instead of becoming upset or giving in to the feelings, the person becomes aware of their feelings and learns to accept the thought and replace it with something positive.

Jean Piaget, a Swiss developmental psychologist, said this:

"If you want to be creative, stay in part a child, with the creativity and invention that characterizes children before they are deformed by adulthood."

Piaget advanced his own theory of cognitive development. His theory identified how cognition changes in each stage associated with age. There are four stages:

- *Sensorimotor stage:* Birth to two years old. At this age, a child learns through senses, touch, movement and manipulation of items and stimuli in the environment.

- *Preoperational stage:* Two to seven years old. At this stage, a child learns though the use of language. Thinking is very concrete and tends to be egocentric.

14

- *Concrete Operational*: Seven to eleven years old: At this age, a child is still very concrete in reasoning, but can use logic to develop solutions and begin to think about outcomes. Thinking still is egocentric.

- *Formal Operational*: Eleven years and older. At this stage, a person begins to think in abstract terms. A person can think of long-term effects, and begins to think more globally. They can formulate ideas regarding morals and ethics, social situations, political situations, and future planning. Their thinking becomes less egocentric and they gain the ability to identify their impact on others.

Piaget's Theory

Stage	Age Range	Description
Sensorimotor	0-2 years	Coordination of senses with motor response, sensory curiosity about the world. Language used for demands and cataloguing. Object permanence developed
Preoperational	2-7 years	Symbolic thinking, use of proper syntax and grammar to express full concepts. Imagination and intuition are strong, but complex abstract thought still difficult. Conservation developed.
Concrete Operational	7-11 years	Concepts attached to concrete situations. Time, space, and quantity are understood and can be applied, but not as independent concepts
Formal Operations	11+	Theoretical, hypothetical, and counterfactual thinking. Abstract logic and reasoning. Strategy and planning become possible. Concepts learned in one context can be applied to another.

The Psychology Notes Headquarter - http://www.PsychologyNotesHQ.com

Piaget also believed people learned about their environment by developing schemas. A schema is a way to categorize knowledge, and it changes with experience. Human beings acquire schemas in three ways:

- **Assimilation:** The process of adding to an existing schema as new stimuli or situations are experienced.

- **Accommodation**: The process of changing our current schema, or the development of an entirely new schema.

- **Equilibration:** The balance between assimilation and accommodation. Equilibration is the balance between applying previous knowledge or assimilation and changing our thoughts or behavior based on new information or accommodation.

DEVELOPMENTAL THEORY

Developmental theories focus on the growth and development of humans at certain ages and across the life span. These theories attempt to explain how a person develops emotionally or psychologically. Some theories believe that the stages of development are continuous, while others feel the stages are discontinuous. Discontinuous would mean a human being could not move past a developmental stage until its issue or crisis was resolved.

Sigmund Freud is the most famous psychologist in history. He said:

"Men are far more moral than they think, and far more immoral than they can imagine.

Freud's development of his theory of psychosexual development was a watershed in human history. Freud believed that human beings possess an inherent sexual energy, which he labeled as libido. Libido, which is present from birth, develops over five stages. Freud believed that personality was developed by the successful completion of these stages and was fully developed by puberty. Freud believed that if a stage was unresolved, the person would be fixated in this stage. He believed fixating would lead to mental disorders, including neurosis in adulthood.

- *Oral stage:* Birth to years one or two. A child is focused on oral gratification with nursing or bottle. The child learns pleasure as well as physical satisfaction (the elimination of hunger) orally. If a child is neglected, or when the child has to wean from the breast or bottle, they become upset. One example of an oral fixation in adulthood is a smoking habit.

- *Anal stage:* One to three years old. A child focuses on gratification through bladder or bowel retention and elimination. A child learns gratification from the ability to independently control physical elimination. Conflict occurs if the child is excessively punished for their inability to control their bowels, or if they are exposed to rigid scheduling. One example of anal fixation is someone who is compulsively clean or neat, in which case they would be known as "anal retentive."

- *Phallic/yonic stage:* Three to six years old. A child focuses on their own genitalia. The child realizes there are difference between males and females. Freud believed that there was a conflict that occurs in this stage that he called the Oedipus complex, where he felt that a child subconsciously longs for the attention of their parent of the opposite sex. This stage is still considered controversial in the psychological world.

- *Latent stage*: Six years old to puberty. This is a time where a child may continue to work towards resolution of the previous stages, or is fairly dormant.

- *Genital stage*: Puberty to death. A person can identify their sexual urges but is able to delay gratification. A person is working on or has established the ability to obtain and maintain relationships that are outside sexual desires as well as friendships.

Stage	Age	Focus of Libido	Development	Adult Fixation
Oral	0 to 1	Mouth, Tongue, Lips	Weaning off of breastfeeding or formula	Smoking, Overeating
Anal	1 to 3	Anus	Toilet training	Orderliness or Messiness
Phallic	3 to 6	Genitalia	Resolving Oedipus/Electra complex	Deviancy, Sexual Dysfunction
Latency	6 to 12	None	Developing defense mechanisms	None
Genital	12 +	Genitals	Full sexual maturity	If all stages are successfully complete, the person should be fully sexually mature and healthy.

Freud is also noted for his theory of the human psyche that includes his theory of development of the id, ego and superego.

- *The Id*: Based on instinct, impulsivity and pleasure. The id demands immediate gratification. The id is not in touch with reality or logic.
- *The Ego*: This part of the psyche attempts to balance the needs of the id and the needs of the superego. The ego is reality-based.
- *The Superego*: This part of the psyche is based on morals and ethics. The superego strives to always do the right thing or not act at all.

Freud also discussed the conscious mind, subconscious mind and the unconscious mind. The conscious mind means you are very aware of your thoughts, memories, and actions. The subconscious mind is just below the conscious mind. Information should be able to be retrieved at this level, but there is something blocking it. The unconscious mind is where thoughts, feelings or information goes when your consciousness can not cope with the information. This can be because it is too traumatic for the psyche to recall.

> Erik Erikson, a developmental psychologist influenced by Freud, said:
>
> *"Man's true taproots are nourished in the sequence of generations, and he loses his taproots in disrupted developmental time, not in abandoned localities."*

In formulating his theory of developmental psychology, Erikson focused on conflicts that take place within the ego, while Freud focused on conflict between the id and ego. Erikson developed the theory of psychosocial development, identifying eight stages through which a human being should pass, from infancy to late adulthood. In each stage the person confronts and hopefully masters new challenges. Each stage builds on the successful completion of earlier stages. The challenges of stages not successfully completed may be expected to reappear as problems in the future. These are Erikson's stages:

- *Hope: Trust vs. Mistrust:* (Infants, 0 to 1 year) The first stage of Erik Erikson's centers around the infant's basic needs being met by the parents. The infant depends on the parents, especially the mother, for food, sustenance, and comfort. The child's relative understanding of world and society come from the parents and their interaction with the child. If the parents expose the child to warmth, regularity, and dependable affection, the infant's view of the world will be one of trust. Should the parents fail to provide a secure environment and to meet the child's basic need a sense of mistrust will result. According to Erikson, the major developmental task in infancy is to learn whether or not other people, especially primary caregivers, regularly satisfy basic needs.

- *Will: Autonomy vs. Shame & Doubt* (Toddlers, 2 to 3 years) As the child gains control over eliminative functions and motor abilities, they begin to explore their surroundings. The parents still provide a strong base of security from which the child can venture out to assert their will. The parents' patience and encouragement helps foster autonomy in the child. Highly restrictive parents, however, are more likely to instill the child with a sense of doubt and reluctance to attempt new challenges. As they gain increased muscular coordination and mobility, toddlers become capable of satisfying some of their own needs.

21

- *Purpose: Initiative vs. Guilt* (Preschool, 4 to 6 years) Initiative adds to autonomy the quality of undertaking, planning and attacking a task for the sake of being active and on the move. The child is learning to master the world around him, learning basic skills and principles of physics. Things fall down, not up. Round things roll. He learns how to zip his pants and tie his shoes, and count and speak with ease. At this stage, the child wants to begin and complete his own actions for a purpose. Guilt is a confusing new emotion. He may feel guilty over things that logically should not cause guilt. He may feel guilt when his initiative does not produce desired results. The development of courage and independence are what set preschoolers, ages three to six years of age, apart from other age groups. Young children in this category face the challenge of initiative versus guilt.

- *Competence: Industry vs. Inferiority* (Childhood, 7 to 12 years) The aim to bring a productive situation to completion gradually supersedes the whims and wishes of play. The fundamentals of technology are developed. To lose the hope of such "industrious" association may pull the child back to the more isolated, less conscious familial rivalry of the Oedipal time.

- *Fidelity: Identity vs. Role Confusion* (Adolescents, 13 to 19 years) The adolescent is newly concerned with how they appear to others. Superego identity is the accrued confidence that the outer sameness and continuity prepared in the future are matched by the sameness and continuity of one's meaning for oneself, as evidenced in the promise of a career. The ability to settle on a school or occupational identity is pleasant. In later stages of adolescence, the child develops a sense of sexual identity.

- *Love: Intimacy vs. Isolation* (Young Adults, 20 to 34 years) The Intimacy vs. Isolation conflict is emphasized around the ages of 20 to 34. At the start of this stage, identity vs. role confusion is coming to an end, though it still lingers at the foundation of the stage. Young adults are still eager to blend their identities with friends and fit in. Erikson believes people are sometimes isolated due to intimacy. We are afraid of rejections such as being turned down or our partners breaking up with us.

- *Care: Generativity vs. Stagnation* (Middle Adulthood, 35 to 65 years) Generativity is the concern of establishing and guiding the next generation. Socially-valued work and disciplines are expressions of generativity. Simply having or wanting children does not, in and of itself, achieve generativity. During middle age, the primary developmental task is one of contributing to society and helping to guide future generations. When a person makes a contribution during this period, perhaps by raising a family or working toward the betterment of society, they achieve generativity.

- *Wisdom: Ego Integrity vs. Despair* (Seniors, 65 years and up) As we grow older and become senior citizens, we tend to slow down our productivity and explore life as a retired person. It is during this time that we contemplate our accomplishments and are able to develop integrity if we see ourselves as having led a successful life. If we see our life as unproductive, or feel that we did not accomplish our life goals, we become dissatisfied with life and develop despair, often leading to depression and hopelessness.

HUMANISTIC PSYCHOLOGY

Humanistic psychology focuses on the overall good of human beings instead of the negativity or mental illness of the individual. This theory believes that all people are innately good. It also stresses the importance of an individual's potential. This theory believes that negative behavior, mental illness and social problems occur when a person responds to the environment in a negative way that deviates from the natural tendency to do good.

Abraham Maslow was a famous humanistic psychologist who said.

Maslow developed the hierarchy of needs. Maslow identified 5 needs.

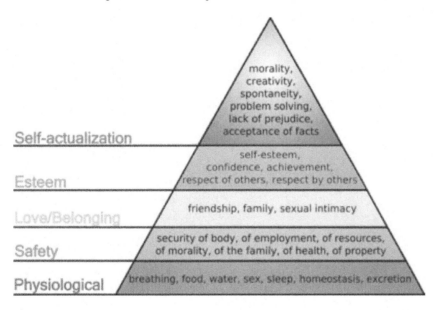

 1. Biological and Physiological: basic physical needs such as food, water, and shelter. It can also include warmth, touch, and sex.

2. Safety needs – Includes protection from the environment. It also includes safety in the sense of financial, legal and emotional stability.

3. Social Needs – This relates to relationships such as family, friends, spouse or significant others and work relationships.

4. Esteem needs – This includes a person's sense of self-esteem and where they view their level of autonomy or accomplishment.

5. Self-Actualization needs – The process of seeking achievement or achieving achievement of one's potential.

II. Personality Theories

Henry Murray and Karen Horney are the two most noted theorists on personality theories. Personality is considered the combination of an individual's unique characteristics. Most people spend a substantial amount of time trying to "figure out" others, including their spouse, friends, children, co-workers and bosses to name a few. These two theories attempt to explain personality.

Henry Murray and Psychogenic Needs

Murray developed a theory of personality that suggests or personality is influenced by our needs. Murray identified these needs as psychogenic needs. These psychogenic needs are at an unconscious level, but it has great impact on our personality. Murray identified two types of needs:

Primary Needs: biological needs such as the need for food, water and shelter

Secondary Needs: psychological or emotional needs, such as the need to be cared for or nurtured, need for independence, and success.

List of Psychogenic Needs

Murray and his colleges identified 24 needs that each person has, but each individual can vary to the level of their own personal need.

1. Ambition Needs

    Achievement: the need to be successful

    Exhibition: to be outwardly successful.

    Recognition: Need to be acknowledged for achievements

2. Materialistic Needs

    Acquisition: Obtaining material items

    Construction: to create items.

    Order: to organize

    Retention: to maintain items.

3. Power Needs

    Abasement: ability to confess or apologize.

Autonomy: ability to independently complete task or manage situation.

Aggression: ability to get above another by attacking or firm stance.

Blame Avoidance: abiding by the rules.

Deference: ability to cooperate.

Dominance: ability to control and lead.

4. Affection Needs

Affiliation: having relationships.

Nurturance: to nurture another.

Play: being able to have fun and enjoy relationships.

Rejection: dismissing others.

Succorance: allowing others to help or protect.

5. Information Needs

Cognizance: asking questions to gain knowledge.

Exposition: educating others, leading others.

Influences on Psychogenic Needs

Murray that needs are multifaceted. They can be interrelated, or support other needs, and they can also conflict with other needs.

Horney's List of Neurotic Needs

Karen Horney is best known for her theory of neurosis. She believed that neurosis was a result of anxiety caused by interpersonal relationships. Her theory proposes that strategies that a person uses to cope with anxiety can appear as a need.

According to Horney, basic anxiety (and therefore neurosis) could result from a variety of things including, " . . . direct or indirect domination, indifference, erratic behavior, lack of respect for the child's individual needs, lack of real guidance, disparaging attitudes, too much admiration or the absence of it, lack of reliable warmth, having to take sides in parental disagreements, too much or too little responsibility, over-protection, isolation from other children, injustice, discrimination, unkept promises, hostile atmosphere, and so on and so on" (Horney, 1945).

These 10 neurotic needs can be classed into three broad categories:

Needs that move you *towards* others.
Individuals to seek validation and acceptance from others but it can be viewed as being "needy"

Needs that move you *away* from others.
This can appear as hostile or antisocial behavior. These individuals are often described as cold, or indifferent.

Needs that move you *against* others.
Takes the form of hostility and is viewed as controlling. These individuals are often described as difficult, mean or controlling.

"Well-adjusted individuals utilize all three of these strategies, shifting focus depending on internal and external factors. So what is it that makes these coping strategies neurotic? According to Horney, it is the overuse of one or more of these interpersonal styles. Neurotic people tend to utilize two or more of these ways of coping, creating conflict, turmoil, and confusion" (Horney, 1945).

In her book **Self-Analysis** (1942), Horney outlined the 10 neurotic needs she had identified:

1. The Neurotic Need for Affection and Approval

This is the need for validation and affection. This is a desire to be liked by others.

2. The Neurotic Need for a Partner Who Will Take Over One's Life

This is a dependent relationship as the person has a deep fear of being abandoned. .

3. The Neurotic Need to Restrict One's Life Within Narrow Borders

This is when a person will ask for very little and become content with status quo.

4. The Neurotic Need for Power

This is when a person must have control, even in situations where it is not necessary. This person has fear of situations where they may find themselves helpless.

5. The Neurotic Need to Exploit Others

This is when a person much manipulate others to obtain their goals. They can exploit others.

6. The Neurotic Need for Prestige

This is when a person must have public acknowledgement. They fear embarrassment and loss of social status.

7. The Neurotic Need for Personal Admiration

This is when a person is narcissistic and wants recognition on who they want others to see them as, and not who they really are. They have an exaggerated sense of self.

8. The Neurotic Need for Personal Achievement

Due to insecurity, these people push themselves to the limits and may not feel satisfied with any level of success.

9. The Neurotic Need for Self-Sufficiency and Independence

The need to be self sufficient may present these persons as "loners".

10. The Neurotic Need for Perfection and Unassailability

This person cannot have any personal flaws and may seek the flaws in others to feel better about themselves.

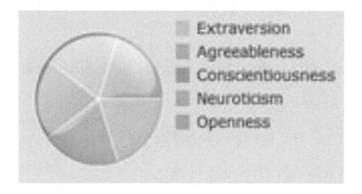

Big Five Dimensions of Personality

Personality researchers have proposed that there are five basic dimensions of personality. Today, many researchers believe that they are five core personality traits. Evidence of this theory has been growing over the past 50 years, beginning with the research of D. W. Fiske (1949) and later expanded upon by other researchers including Norman (1967), Smith (1967), Goldberg (1981), and McCrae & Costa (1987).

The five categories are:

Extraversion: This trait includes characteristics such as excitability, sociability, talkativeness, assertiveness and high amounts of emotional expressiveness.

Agreeableness: This personality dimension includes attributes such as trust, altruism, kindness, affection, and other prosocial behaviors.

Conscientiousness: Common features of this dimension include high levels of thoughtfulness, with good impulse control and goal-directed behaviors. Those high in conscientiousness tend to be organized and mindful of details.

Neuroticism: Individuals high in this trait tend to experience emotional instability, anxiety, moodiness, irritability, and sadness.

Openness: This trait features characteristics such as imagination and insight, and those high in this trait also tend to have a broad range of interests.

Borderline Personality Theory

Marsha Linehan created a bio-social theory regarding borderline personality disorder. Her method of treating Borderline Personality Therapy called Dialectical Behavioral Therapy (DBT). She believed that a person develops this disorder due to environmental situations that occur while a child is growing up. Linehan called this the ***Invalidating Environment***. According to the theory, a person who is emotionally vulnerable has an excessive autonomic nervous system response to stress. This level of distress causes an irrational behavioral and emotional response. This response is due to the lack of ability to have emotional regulation. This is called "emotional dysregulation".

There are 4 key Skills trained in DBT:

Core mindfulness skills: A person becomes more aware of their current thoughts and feelings, and is able to experience the moment.

Interpersonal effectiveness skills:. A person learns how to relate to others without the need to be dramatic, over-attached and ability to ask for what they are really seeking.

Emotion modulation skills: A person learns how to manage their moods and control them to have a more positive outcome.

Distress tolerance skills: A person learns how to manage situations, outcomes and feelings that have negative outcomes.

Learning Theories

Learning theories look at how people learn and obtain new information or knowledge.

David Kolb's model of learning styles is one of the best-known. He believed that individual learning styles evolve from personal genetics, as well as the environment.

Kolb identified 4 learning styles:

The Converger: high ability in Abstract Conceptualization and Active Experimentation. They are highly skilled in the practical application of ideas.

The Diverger: high ability in Concrete Experience and Reflective Observation. They tend to look at the "big picture" and organizing smaller bits of information into a meaningful whole. They tend to be emotional and creative.

The Assimilator: high ability in Abstract Conceptualization and Reflective Observation. Understanding and creating theoretical models is one of their greatest strengths. Assimilators often have jobs in planning and research.

The Accommodator: high ability in Concrete Experience and Active Experimentation. Accommodators are doers; they enjoy performing experiments and carrying out plans in the real world. Out of all four learning styles, Accommodators tend to be the greatest risk-takers.

Intelligence theories

Charles Spearman - General Intelligence: Also known as the "g factor", is the belief that intelligence could be measured and scored.

Louis L. Thurstone - Primary Mental Abilities: theory states that there are seven primary mental abilities. These abilities are:

Verbal comprehension

Reasoning

Perceptual speed

Numerical ability

Word fluency

Associative memory

Spatial visualization

Howard Gardner - Multiple Intelligences: believed that identifying a person's intelligence by a score was not the best way to measure intelligence. He identified 8 types of intelligence.

The eight intelligences are:

Visual-spatial Intelligence

Verbal-linguistic Intelligence

Bodily-kinesthetic Intelligence

Logical-mathematical Intelligence

Interpersonal Intelligence

Musical Intelligence

Intra personal Intelligence

Naturalistic Intelligence

Robert Sternberg - Triarchic Theory of Intelligence: defined intelligence as "mental activity directed toward purposive adaptation to, selection and shaping of, real-world environments relevant to one's life." He viewed intelligence as talents. He believed intelligence had 3 factors.

Analytical intelligence: This component refers to problem-solving abilities.

Creative intelligence: This aspect of intelligence involves the ability to deal with new situations using past experiences and current skills.

Practical intelligence: This element refers to the ability to adapt to a changing environment.

Social Learning Theory

Bandura created a social learning theory. He believed that there was a social element to learning, which included that people learn behaviors by watching other people interact. This is known as modeling. Bandura social learning theory indicated that not all behavior is through observation. There are also other ways to learn behavior. Bandura described learning through attention, retention, reproduction, motivation.

There are three core concepts:

1. People can learn through observation.

Bandura had a famous study that demonstrated that children learn and imitate behaviors they observe. Bandura identified three models of observational learning which are:

A live model, where the individual demonstrates the behavior.

A verbal instructional model, where the individual describes or instructs.

A symbolic model, which involves real or fictional characters displaying behaviors in books, films, television programs, or online media.

2. Mental states are important to learning.

Intrinsic Reinforcement

Bandura believed that intrinsic reinforcement also effects learning. Bandura defined intrinsic reinforcement as a form of internal reward, such as pride, satisfaction, and a sense of accomplishment.

3. Learning does not necessarily lead to a change in behavior.

People can learn without demonstration or observation.

The Modeling Process

Sometimes, observed behaviors are not effectively learned. Factors involving both the person demonstrating and the person learning can play a role in whether social learning is successful. Bandura believed there needed to be certain steps in the observational learning and modeling process:

Attention: Appropriate attention is needed to effectively learn through observation. If the person is distracted, they may miss important information or steps in the process

Retention: The person needs to be able to retain the information learned

Reproduction: The person needs to be able to reproduce the behavior that was observed. Reproduction leads to practice, which them leads to acquirement of the skill.

Motivation: The person also has to be motivated to learn and to use the new skills. . <u>Reinforcement</u> and <u>punishment</u> play an important role in motivation

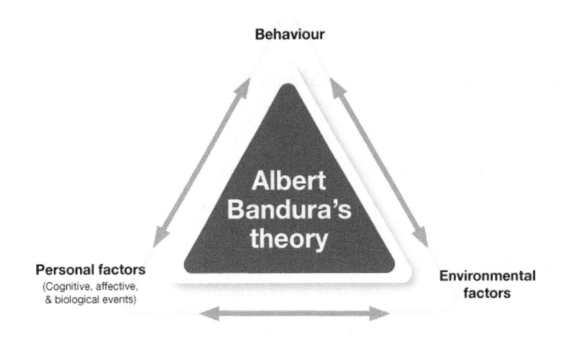

<u>Social Psychology</u>

Social Psychology is the study of how people interact with others in a social setting, in relationships (personal and professional) and how our attitudes and beliefs are shaped by cultural norms. <u>Gordon Allport</u> is noted for his theory on social psychology. He describes social psychology as a scientific method "to understand and explain how the thought, feeling and behavior of individuals are influenced by the actual, imagined or implied presence of other human beings" (1985). There are many phenomena that ae explained by social psychology.

Actor Observer Bias: a tendency to attribute one's own actions to external causes, while attributing other people's behaviors to internal causes. This is most commonly seen when the outcome is negative. For example: Jessica and Mary and Sam are up for the same promotion. Jessica does not get the promotion. She may believe that she did not get it because of factors due to not being at the job long enough (external cause), where she may feel Sam did not get the promotion because he does not get along well with others or does not know his job well enough (internal cause).

The Bystander Effect: The phenomenon in which the greater the number of people present, the less likely people are to help a person in distress. When an emergency situation occurs, observers are more likely to take action if there are few or no other witnesses. This is because each individual believes someone else will take a leadership role or will take action and that they do not have to. This is known as diffusion of responsibility.   This is why a person is more likely to act when they are alone or with only a few, since it would imply they are the only ones who could help.

Attachment theory

 John Bowlby developed the theory of attachment. Attachment is the bond between people. Bowlby described attachment as "lasting psychological connectedness between human beings."

Bowlby believed that the bonds formed in infancy to their caregivers have a tremendous impact that continues throughout the child's life. Attachment theory states that when a caregiver is emotionally available and is responsive to a child's needs, the child learns to feel secure. This security leads to the child's ability to become autonomous and secure in their relationships with others.

Ainsworth conducted a study based on Bowlby's theory of attachment. In the study, researchers observed toddlers between the ages of 12 and 18 months as they responded to a situation in which they were briefly left alone and then reunited with their mothers. Based upon the outcome of the study, Ainsworth described three major styles of attachment:

Secure attachment: The child becomes upset when the caregiver leaves, and experiences happiness when they return. While they become upset with the removal of the caregiver, they have a positive attachment and soon learns that the caregiver will return. They are able to turn to their caregiver for their physical and emotional needs and the caregiver is able to satisfy these needs.

Ambivalent-insecure attachment: the level of distress that a child experiences when the caregiver leaves is very high and atypical. The child cannot be consoled. This is usually seen in infants and children where the caregiver has not been able to consistently provide for the needs of the child.

Avoidant-insecure attachment: The child shows no preference to the caregiver or a stranger. They do not demonstrate distress upon the caregiver leaving and do not exhibit joy upon their return. This pattern is most often seen in children who have been abused or severely neglected.

An additional type was added later: disorganized attachment: a display of confusing mix of behavior and the child may both avoid or resist the parent. There seems to be a clear lack of attachment.

The Stages of Attachment

Rudolph Schaffer and Peggy Emerson completed a longitudinal study with 60 infants. The study analyzed the number of attachment relationships that infants form. The infants were observed every four weeks during the first year of life, and then once again at 18 months. Based on the outcomes, they identified four distinct phases of attachment.

Pre-attachment Stage: From birth to three months, there is not a particular attachment to a specific caregiver. A caregiver usually provides at an infant's natural signals.

Indiscriminate Attachment: From around six weeks of age to seven months, infants start to demonstrate a desire for primary and secondary caregivers. During this phase, infants begin to develop an attachment to their caregivers. They develop a feeling of trust that the caregiver will respond to their needs

Discriminate Attachment: From about seven to eleven months of age, an infant's attachment to one specific caregiver is clearly observed. The infant will show distress when separated from caregiver. They also can show anxiety around strangers.

Multiple Attachments: After approximately nine months of age, children begin to attach to others including other caregivers, other children, other family, etc.

When there is a problem with attachment:

Lack of a secure attachment can lead to many mental health issues including oppositional-defiant disorder (ODD), conduct disorder (CD) or borderline personality disorder. Research also suggests that children adopted after the age of six months have a higher risk of attachment problems. Children who do not have a sense of healthy attachment can also have trouble with their adult relationships.

Abnormal Psychology

Abnormal Psychology is identification, treatment and understanding of abnormal behavior and psychopathology. The term covers a broad range of disorders, from depression to obsession-compulsion to sexual deviation. Counselors, clinical psychologists, social workers and psychiatrists work directly in this field.

Perspectives in Abnormal Psychology

There are 3 aspects in viewing mental health. Many mental health professionals may use 1 or all 3 aspects in order to appropriately diagnose and treat mental health disorders.

Behavioral: The behavioral approach to abnormal psychology focuses on observable behaviors. In behavioral therapy, the approach looks at the behaviors and not the underlying cause.

Medical: The medical approach to abnormal psychology focuses on the biological causes on mental illness. This perspective emphasizes understanding the underlying cause of disorders, which might include genetic inheritance, related physical disorders, infections and chemical imbalances. Medications may be use alone or in conjunction to therapy.

Cognitive: The cognitive approach to abnormal psychology focuses on how internal thoughts, perceptions and reasoning contribute to psychological disorders. Cognitive behavioral therapy focuses on thoughts, feelings and behaviors.

Types of Psychological Disorders

Psychological disorders are defined as patterns of behavioral or psychological symptoms that impact multiple areas of life. Mental health professionals use The *Diagnostic and Statistical Manual of Mental Disorders* (DSM V) published by the American Psychiatric Association to identify and diagnose mental health diagnosis. Categories of psychological disorders include:

Adjustment Disorders

Mood Disorders

Anxiety Disorders

Developmental Disorders

DSM V

The DSM V uses a multiaxial approach to diagnosing.

<u>Axis I: Clinical Syndromes</u>

Mental health diagnosis

<u>Axis II: Developmental Disorders and Personality Disorders</u>

Developmental disorders include autism and mental retardation diagnosis

Personality disorder diagnosis: clinical diagnosis that addresses if a person has a maladaptive way of interacting with the world (ex: Paranoid, Antisocial, and Borderline Personality Disorders)

Axis III: Physical Conditions

Any medical condition that is chronic (Obesity, Diabetes, AIDS)

Axis IV: Severity of Psychosocial Stressors

Events in a persons life, such as divorce, death of a loved one, starting a new job, loss of a job, etc..

Axis V: Global Assessment of Functioning (GAF)

On the final axis, the clinician rates the person's level of functioning both at the present time and the highest level within the previous year. This helps the clinician understand how the above four axes are affecting the person and what type of changes could be expected.

<u>GAF SCALE for Adults</u>

91 - 100 No symptoms. Superior functioning in a wide range of activities, life's problems never seem to get out of hand, is sought out by others because of his or her many positive qualities.

81 - 90 Absent or minimal symptoms (e.g., mild anxiety before an exam), good functioning in all areas, interested and involved in a wide range of activities, socially effective, generally satisfied with life, no more than everyday problems or concerns (e.g., an occasional argument with family members).

71 - 80 If symptoms are present, they are transient and expectable reactions to psychosocial stressors (e.g., difficulty concentrating after family argument); no more than slight impairment in social, occupational, or school functioning (e.g., temporarily falling behind in schoolwork).

61 - 70 Some mild symptoms (e.g., depressed mood and mild insomnia) *or* some difficulty in social, occupational, or school functioning (e.g., occasional truancy, or theft within the household), but generally functioning pretty well, has some meaningful interpersonal relationships.

51 - 60 Moderate symptoms (e.g., flat affect and circumlocutory speech, occasional panic attacks) *or* moderate difficulty in social, occupational, or school functioning (e.g., few friends, conflicts with peers or co-workers).

41 - 50 Serious symptoms (e.g., suicidal ideation, severe obsessional rituals, frequent shoplifting) *or* any serious impairment in social, occupational, or school functioning (e.g., no friends, unable to keep a job, cannot work).

31 - 40 Some impairment in reality testing or communication (e.g., speech is at times illogical, obscure, or irrelevant) *or* major impairment in several areas, such as work or school, family relations, judgment, thinking, or mood (e.g., depressed adult avoids friends, neglects family, and is unable to work; child frequently beats up younger children, is defiant at home, and is failing at school).

21 - 30 Behavior is considerably influenced by delusions or hallucinations *or* serious impairment, in communication or judgment (e.g., sometimes incoherent, acts grossly inappropriately, suicidal preoccupation) *or* inability to function in almost all areas (e.g., stays in bed all day, no job, home, or friends)

11 - 20 Some danger of hurting self or others (e.g., suicide attempts without clear expectation of death; frequently violent; manic excitement) *or* occasionally fails to maintain minimal personal hygiene (e.g., smears feces) *or* gross impairment in communication (e.g., largely incoherent or mute).

1 - 10 Persistent danger of severely hurting self or others (e.g., recurrent violence) *or* persistent inability to maintain minimal personal hygiene *or* serious suicidal act with clear expectation of death.

0 Inadequate information

GAF for Children

100-91 Superior functioning in all areas (at home, at school and with peers); involved in a wide range of activities and has many interests (e.g., has hobbies or participates in extracurricular activities or belongs to an organized group such as Scouts, etc.); likeable, confident; 'everyday' worries never get out of hand; doing well in school; no symptoms.

90-81 Good functioning in all areas; secure in family, school, and with peers; there may be transient difficulties and 'everyday' worries that occasionally get out of hand (e.g., mild anxiety associated with an important exam, occasional 'blowups' with siblings, parents or peers).

80-71 No more than slight impairments in functioning at home, at school, or with peers; some disturbance of behavior or emotional distress may be present in response to life stresses (e.g., parental separations, deaths, birth of a sibling), but these are brief and interference with functioning is transient; such children are only minimally disturbing to others and are not considered deviant by those who know them.

70-61 Some difficulty in a single area but generally functioning well (e.g., sporadic or isolated antisocial acts, such as occasionally playing hooky or petty theft; consistent minor difficulties with school work; mood changes of brief duration; fears and anxieties which do not lead to gross avoidance behaviour; self-doubts); has some meaningful interpersonal relationships; most people who do not know the child well would not consider him/her deviant but those who do know him/her well might express concern.

60-51 Variable functioning with sporadic difficulties or symptoms in several but not all social areas; disturbance would be apparent to those who encounter the child in a dysfunctional setting or time but not to those who see the child in other settings.

50-41 Moderate degree of interference in functioning in most social areas or severe impairment of functioning in one area, such as might result from, for example, suicidal preoccupations and ruminations, school refusal and other forms of anxiety, obsessive rituals, major conversion symptoms, frequent anxiety attacks, poor to inappropriate social skills, frequent episodes of aggressive or other antisocial behaviour with some preservation of meaningful social relationships.

40-31 Major impairment of functioning in several areas and unable to function in one of these areas i.e., disturbed at home, at school, with peers, or in society at large, e.g., persistent aggression without clear instigation; markedly withdrawn and isolated behaviour due to either mood or thought disturbance, suicidal attempts with clear lethal intent; such children are likely to require special schooling and/or hospitalisation or withdrawal from school (but this is not a sufficient criterion for inclusion in this category).

30-21 Unable to function in almost all areas e.g., stays at home, in ward, or in bed all day without taking part in social activities or severe impairment in reality testing or serious impairment in communication (e.g., sometimes incoherent or inappropriate).

20-11 Needs considerable supervision to prevent hurting others or self (e.g., frequently violent, repeated suicide attempts) or to maintain personal hygiene or gross impairment in all forms of communication, e.g., severe abnormalities in verbal and gestural communication, marked social aloofness, stupor, etc.

10-1 Needs constant supervision (24-hour care) due to severely aggressive or self-destructive behavior or gross impairment in reality testing, communication, cognition, affect or personal hygiene.

<u>List of Psychological Disorders</u>

Mood Disorders: The disorders are characterized by disturbance of mood as a predominant feature.   EX: Depression, bi-polar and mania

Depression is most commonly associate with feeling of deep sadness, lack of energy, marked tearfulness or crying and in some cases, suicidal thoughts or actions.

According to Mayo Clinic, (http://www.mayoclinic.com/health/depression/DS00175)

Depression symptoms include:

- Feelings of sadness
- Irritability, easily agitated
- Loss of interest or pleasure in activities that use to bring them joy
- Decrease in sex drive
- Change in sleep pattern either trouble sleeping or too much sleep
- Changes in appetite wither increase or decrease
- Difficulty sitting still
- Easily angered
- Decrease in cognitive abilities
- Difficulty in concentration
- Loss of energy, difficulty having energy to complete tasks
- Feelings of worthlessness or guilt
- Thoughts of dying or suicide
- Easily tearful or easy to cry
- Unexplained physical problems, including headaches or general pain

For some people, depression symptoms are so severe that it's obvious something isn't right. Other people feel generally miserable or unhappy without really knowing why.

Bipolar disorder:

The three types of bipolar disorder:

Bipolar 1 Disorder, in which the primary symptom presentation is manic, or rapid (daily) cycling episodes of mania and depression.

Bipolar 2 Disorder, in which the primary symptom presentation is recurrent depression accompanied by hypomanic episodes (a milder state of mania in which the symptoms are not severe enough to cause marked impairment in social or occupational functioning or need for hospitalization, but are sufficient to be observable by others).

Cyclothymic Disorder, a chronic state of cycling between hypomanic and depressive episodes that do not reach the diagnostic standard for bipolar disorder (APA, 2000, pp. 388–392).

Manic episodes are characterized by:

A distinct period of abnormally and persistently elevated, expansive, or irritable mood, lasting at least 1 week (or any duration if hospitalization is necessary)

During the period of mood disturbance, three (or more) of the following symptoms have persisted (4 if the mood is only irritable) and have been present to a significant degree:

increased self-esteem or grandiosity, decreased need for sleep (e.g., feels rested after only 3 hours of sleep), more talkative than usual or pressure to keep talking, flight of ideas or subjective experience that thoughts are racing distractibility (i.e., attention too easily drawn to unimportant or irrelevant external stimuli), increase in goal-directed activity (either socially, at work or school, or sexually) or psychomotor agitation, excessive involvement in pleasurable activities that have a high potential for painful consequences (e.g., engaging in unrestrained buying sprees, sexual indiscretions, or foolish business investments)" (APA, 2000, p. 362).

(http://www.mayoclinic.com/health/depression/DS00175)

According to Wikipedia. Suicide "is the act of intentionally causing one's own death. Suicide is often committed out of despair, the cause of which is frequently attributed to a mental disorder such as depression, bipolar disorder, schizophrenia, borderline personality disorder, alcoholism, or drug abuse. Stress factors such as financial difficulties or troubles with interpersonal relationships often play a role. Efforts to prevent suicide include limiting access to firearms, treating mental illness and drug misuse, and improving economic development. The most commonly used method of suicide varies by country and is partly related to availability. Common methods include: hanging, pesticide poisoning, and firearms. Around 800,000 to a million people die by suicide every year, making it the 10th leading cause of death worldwide. Rates are higher in men than in women, with males three to four times more likely to kill themselves than females. There are an estimated 10 to 20 million non-fatal attempted suicides every year. Attempts are more common in young people and females".

There is a myth that talking to a person about suicidal thoughts causes the person to think about or act on suicidal thoughts. For many years this was a concern for therapists.

THIS IS NOT TRUE. A person who is thinking or planning suicide will not be persuaded to act by discussing the topic of suicide. In fact, a person who is thinking about suicide may use the opportunity to be talked OUT of planning or the attempt. This is the basis of the origination of suicide hotlines. As a therapist, there is a need to constantly assess a persons suicidal thoughts and plans.

46

Anxiety Disorders: Anxiety disorders have the presence of fears or phobias, constant worry and nervousness, can also have physical complaints without medical reasoning, and can interfere with daily living.   EX: Panic attack, agoraphobia, obsessive-compulsive and post traumatic stress disorder.

According to the DSM V the diagnostic criteria for anxiety disorders includes:

(1) Distress that is marked and excessive for what would be expected from the stressor and

(2) Creates significant impairment in school, work or social environments.

In addition to these requirements, the symptoms must occur within three months of exposure to the stressor, the symptoms must not meet the criteria for an Axis I or Axis II disorder, the symptoms must not be related to bereavement and the symptoms must not last for longer than six months after exposure to the stressor.

Adjustment Disorders: The key symptoms of adjustment disorders is the development of symptoms due to a known stressor. There is a known environmental, situational, or even medical reason for the change in feelings and/or behavior.

In order to have the diagnosis of adjustment disorder, the symptoms must appear within 3 months of the stressful event. Any type of stress can trigger an adjustment disorder, such as:

- Divorce or other relationship break-up
- A car accident, can even be a small accident
- A significant loss due to death
- A serious medical diagnosis, such as cancer
- Any major life transition or change that can include a move, a marriage or having a baby
- Living through or being impacted by a natural disaster

Sometimes an adjustment disorder develops due to a combination or stressors, or an ongoing stressor that does not have a designated end date.

In order to qualify for the diagnosis, the symptoms of an adjustment disorder must decrease within 6 months after the stressful event occurred.

Psychotic Disorders: This group of disorders is include symptoms of delusions, hallucinations, disorganized behavior and impairment in reality testing. EX: Schizophrenia, schizoaffective disorder and schizophreniform

The sufferer must have one of the following symptoms:

- delusions,
- hallucinations,
- grossly disorganized or catatonic behavior,
- or disorganized speech.

Developmental Disorders: Is attributable to a mental or physical impairment or combination of mental and physical impairments; manifested before the individual attains age 22; will always be present; results in substantial functional limitations in three or more of the following areas of major life activity; Self-care; Receptive and expressive language; Learning; Mobility; Self-direction; Capacity for independent living; and Economic self-sufficiency.

The following is a list of developmental disabilities: Mental retardation, in which victims have lower intelligence levels than average; Down Syndrome means a set of mental and physical characteristics related to having an additional copy of Chromosome 21; Fragile X Syndrome which is caused by a deficiency in a particular part of the Fragile X; Angelman's Syndrome with marked physical and mental characteristics, Autism, Asperger's Syndrome, People on the autism spectrum have difficulties in verbal and non-verbal communication, social interactions, and leisure activities. The severity of this condition may vary from mild to severe, Williams Syndrome find it difficult to see spatial relationships between objects around them, phenylketonuria (PKU) is a metabolic syndrome, and cerebral palsy which effects fine and gross motor development and movement and epilepsy which is a siezre disorder.

- **Intellectual Disabilities**

Mild Intellectual Disabilities: IQ level 50-55 to 70

Moderate Intellectual Disabilities: IQ level 35-40 to 50-55

Severe Intellectual Disabilities: IQ level 20-25 to 35-40

Profound Intellectual Disabilities: IQ level below 20 or 25

The mild range pertains to the mental equivalent of an 8-12 year old child.

The moderate range means mental age of a 5-8 years old.

Severe is mental age of 1-4 years to.

Profound is infantile state.

There are many people with mild or moderate intellectual disabilities that live on their own and hold gainful employment. A person with an intellectual disability may have limited ability to communicate, difficulty with ability to completeactivities of daily living, and difficulty comprehending social cues. They may also have limitations on solving problems and the consequences to their actions.   May have other disabilities as well.

General Things to Remember: Mental retardation is **NOT** a disease and it is **NOT** mental illness. Persons with MR are individuals and have varying strengths, interests, and personalities and have the ability to learn, develop and grow. People with MR may need more time to learn tasks.

Impulse-Control Disorders

Impulse-control disorders are those that involve an inability to control impulses, resulting in harm to oneself or others. This disorder is also often associated with persons who have legal involvement or have issues in school (if school-aged child). Impulse-control disorders are thought to have both neurological and environmental causes and are known to be exacerbated by stress . Some mental health professionals regard several of these disorders, such as compulsive gambling or shopping, as addictions. In impulse-control disorder, the impulse action is typically preceded by feelings of tension and excitement and followed by a sense of relief and gratification, often—but not always— accompanied by guilt or remorse.

Types of impulse-control disorders include:

Kleptomania (stealing)

Pyromania (fire-starting)

Trichotillomania (hair-pulling)

Pathological gambling

Intermittent explosive disorder

Dermatillomania (skin-picking)

Also, repetitive self injurious behavior.

Mental Disorders Due to a General Medical Condition

This type of psychological disorder is caused by an underlying medical condition. Medical conditions can cause psychological symptoms such as catatonia and personality changes. Examples of mental disorders due to a general medical condition include:

Psychotic disorder due to epilepsy

Depression caused by diabetes

AIDS related psychosis

Personality changes due to brain damage

Neurocognitive Disorders

These psychological disorders are those that involve cognitive abilities such as memory, problem solving and perception. Some anxiety disorder, mood disorders and psychotic disorders are classified as cognitive disorders. Types of cognitive disorders include:

Alzheimer's disease

Delirium

Dementia

Amnesia

Alzheimer's is the most common form of dementia. This disease effects memory and other intellectual functioning. It interferes with a person's ability to independently manage their daily life. Alzheimer's disease accounts for 50 to 80 percent of dementia cases. According to the Alzheimer Association, "**Alzheimer's is not a normal part of aging**, although the greatest known risk factor is increasing age, and the majority of people with Alzheimer's are 65 and older. But Alzheimer's is not just a disease of old age. Up to 5 percent of people with the disease have early onset Alzheimer's (also known as younger-onset), which often appears when someone is in their 40s or 50s". (http://www.alz.org).

Personality Disorders

Axis II of a diagnosis is for those with developmental disabilities or personality disorders. There are 3 types of personality disorders: Eccentric, Dramatic, and Anxious.

Eccentric Personality Disorders. These people often appear strange or peculiar to others. Their behavior can appear more like someone with psychosis.

Paranoid Personality Disorder – individual generally tends to interpret the actions of others as threatening.

Schizoid Personality Disorder – individual generally detached from social relationships, and shows a narrow range of emotional expression in various social settings.

Schizotypal Personality Disorder – individual is uncomfortable in close relationships, has thought or perceptual distortions, and peculiarities of behavior.

Dramatic Personality Disorders. These people have intense emotional mood swings. There mood liability can be unpredictable. They also tend to have a very distorted perception of themselves and can have very impulsive behaviors that can be dangerous or self-destructive.

Antisocial Personality Disorder – individual shows a pervasive disregard for, and violation of, the rights of others.

Borderline Personality Disorder – individual shows a generalized pattern of instability in interpersonal relationships, self-image, and observable emotions, and significant impulsiveness.

Histrionic Personality Disorder - individual often displays excessive emotionality and attention seeking in various contexts. They tend to overreact to other people, and are often perceived as shallow and self-centered.

Narcissistic Personality Disorder – individual has a grandiose view of themselves, a need for admiration, and a lack of empathy that begins by early adulthood and is present in various situations. These individuals are very demanding in their relationships.

Anxious Personality Disorders. These people are often fearful and anxious about multiple things, persons, or situations. Their anxiety results in strained relationships and odd patterns of behaviors.

Avoidant Personality Disorder – individual is socially inhibited, feels inadequate, and is oversensitive to criticism

Dependent Personality Disorder – individual shows an extreme need to be taken care of that leads to fears of separation, and passive and clinging behavior.

<u>Obsessive-Compulsive Personality Disorder</u> – individual is preoccupied with orderliness, perfectionism, and control at the expense of flexibility, openness, and efficiency.

A little more on Borderline Personality Disorder:

According to the DSM IV TR, BPD is manifested by a pervasive pattern of instability of interpersonal relationships, self-image, and affects, and marked impulsivity beginning by early adulthood and present in a variety of contexts, as indicated by five (or more) of the following:

1. Frantic efforts to avoid real or imagined abandonment. Note: Do not include suicidal or self-mutilating behavior covered in (5).
2. A pattern of unstable and intense interpersonal relationships characterized by alternating between extremes of idealization and devaluation. This is called "splitting."
3. Identity disturbance: markedly and persistently unstable self-image or sense of self.
4. Impulsivity in at least two areas that are potentially self-damaging (e.g., spending, sex, substance abuse, reckless driving, binge eating). Note: Do not include suicidal or self-mutilating behavior covered in (5).
5. Recurrent suicidal behavior, gestures, or threats, or self-mutilating behavior.
6. Affective instability due to a marked reactivity of mood (e.g., intense episodic dysphoria, irritability, or anxiety usually lasting a few hours and only rarely more than a few days).
7. Chronic feelings of emptiness.
8. Inappropriate, intense anger or difficulty controlling anger (e.g., frequent displays of temper, constant anger, recurrent physical fights).
9. Transient, stress-related paranoid ideation or severe dissociative symptoms.

Substance use Disorders

There has been a change in diagnosing substance abuse and dependence since May 2013 and the origination of the DSM V. Currently, The DSM-V recognizes substance related disorders resulting from the use of ten separate classes of drugs: alcohol, caffeine, cannabis, hallucinogens (phencyclidine or similarly acting arylcyclohexylamines), other hallucinogens such as LSD, inhalants, opioids, sedatives, hypnotics, anxiolytics, stimulants (including amphetamine-type substances, cocaine, and other stimulants), tobacco, and other or unknown substances. Therefore, while some major grouping of psychoactive substances are specifically identified, use of other or unknown substances can also form the basis of a substance related or addictive disorder. Substance use disorders span a wide variety of problems arising from substance use, and cover 11 different criteria:

1. Taking more of the substance when you use or using more frequently
2. The desire to cut down the amount or stop using, but not having the ability to be successful.
3. Spending time obtaining, using or recovering from use
4. Experiencing cravings to use
5. Difficulty completing tasks or responsibilities, such as work, home or school, because of use
6. Use continues despite causing conflict in relationships
7. Not attending important social, occupational or recreational activities and using or recovering from us instead
8. Continued use despite the consequences or danger
9. Recognizing there is a physical or psychological addiction, but continuing use anyway.
10. Need for more to get desired effect
11. Use of substances to eliminate withdrawal symptoms.

Case Study: Application of knowledge of Psychology

A 6 month old child begins to cry whenever separated from its mother. The child can be consoled after a few minutes. The child is able to participate in normal activity until the return of his mother. When his mother returns he is very happy and greets her warmly. This behavior is consistent with which theory?

a. Personality Theory
b. Behavioral theory
c. *Attachment Theory*
d. Abnormal Psychology Theory

This would be an example of secure attachment: **Secure attachment**: The child becomes upset when the caregiver leaves, and experiences happiness when they return. While they become upset with the removal of the caregiver, they have a positive attachment and soon learns that the caregiver will return. They are able to turn to their caregiver for their physical and emotional needs and the caregiver is able to satisfy these needs.

A 6 month old child begins to cry whenever separated from its mother. The child becomes so upset, he begins to hyper-ventilate. The child only becomes calm when the mother is present. According to attachment theory, what type of attachment is the child showing.

a. Secure attachment
b. Ambivalent-insecure attachment
c. Avoidant-insecure attachment
d. Disorganized attachment

If the child were unable to be consoled, we would consider the child to have ambivalent-insecure attachment. **Ambivalent-insecure attachment**: the level of distress that a child experiences when the caregiver leaves is very high and atypical. The child cannot be consoled. This is usually seen in infants and children where the caregiver has not been able to consistently provide for the needs of the child.

Suzi is a client that continues to voice concern that she feels she wants a man to become close to her but struggles when they do. She has described several incidents where she has become very overwhelmed and acted in ways that actually push men away. This behavior has been a pattern for many years. This pattern of intense behavior has called her to call off 2 engagements and 1 engagement to be called off by a potential spouse. What is a possible initial diagnosis?

a. Mood Disorder
b. Bipolar disorder
c. Social Phobia
d. Borderline Personality Disorder

Borderline personality has characteristics of difficulty obtaining and maintaining relationships, especially those with intimacy; difficulty with self image, difficulty with mood stability, and intense fear of abandonment.

A person with BPD often does not recognize that they engange in pushing the person (love object) away, when what they desperately want is to have that person close. Their inability to manage their moods and their deep fears cause this phenomena. They then feel what they fear the most: abandonment.

Joey has an intellectual disability. His FSIQ is 40. He often becomes physically aggressive whenever there is any change. A staff has resigned after 10 years of working with him. What would be the proper protocol for helping Joey to adjust to the change?

a. Tell Joey the day of the change in staff
b. Have the new staff be introduced by his current staff for a few days before to help with the transition
c. Have the current staff tell Joey everyday that she is leaving to help him acclimate
d. Don't tell Joey information because it may upset him, but tell his parents so they are aware

Transition is often difficult for many people. This is especially true for those with intellectual disabilities. Joey may have difficulty expressing his sadness at the loss of his staff. He may also have feelings of fear about the new staff that will replace his old staff. Transitioning Joey will help to decrease negative behaviors. It can also help Joey to learn how to express his feelings. Lastly it will help him adjust to the change.

You have a client that comes to you because their spouse of 20 years has passed away 2 months ago. She complains of feeling sad, cries often, has difficulty completing tasks and has trouble going to work and has called in 10 times during the past 2 months. The proper diagnosis at this time is?

a. Major Depression
b. Adjustment Disorder
c. Psychosis
d. Mood Disorder NOS

Adjustment Disorders: The key symptoms of adjustment disorders is the development of symptoms due to a known stressor. There is a known environmental, situational, or even medical reason for the change in feelings and/or behavior.

In order to have the diagnosis of adjustment disorder, the symptoms must appear within 3 months of the stressful event. Any type of stress can trigger an adjustment disorder, such as:

- Divorce or other relationship break-up
- A car accident, can even be a small accident
- A significant loss due to death
- A serious medical diagnosis, such as cancer
- Any major life transition or change that can include a move, a marriage or having a baby
- Living through or being impacted by a natural disaster

Sometimes an adjustment disorder develops due to a combination or stressors, or an ongoing stressor that does not have a designated end date.

In order to qualify for the diagnosis, the symptoms of an adjustment disorder must decrease within 6 months after the stressful event

Adjustment disorders can often be treated with cognitive behavioral therapy in individual and/or group sessions.

You have a client that comes to you because their spouse of 20 years has passed away 1 year ago. She complains of feeling depressed, cries all the time, feels like she can talk to him and see him, has difficulty completing tasks and has trouble going to work and has called in 10 times during the past 2 months. And often thinks of suicide. The proper diagnosis at this time is?

a. Major Depression
b. Adjustment Disorder
c. Psychosis
d. Major Depression with Suicidal features

- Feelings of sadness
- Irritability, easily agitated
- Loss of interest or pleasure in activities that use to bring them joy
- Decrease in sex drive
- Change in sleep pattern either trouble sleeping or too much sleep
- Changes in appetite wither increase or decrease
- Difficulty sitting still
- Easily angered
- Decrease in cognitive abilities
- Difficulty in concentration
- Loss of energy, difficulty having energy to complete tasks
- Feelings of worthlessness or guilt
- Thoughts of dying or suicide
- Easily tearful or easy to cry

Same scenario: You have a client that comes to you because their spouse of 20 years has passed away 1 year ago. She complains of feeling depressed, cries all the time, feels like she can talk to him and see him, has difficulty completing tasks and has trouble going to work and has called in 10 times during the past 2 months. And often thinks of suicide. This is your first session with the client. What should you address first?

a. The call ins to work
b. The constant crying
c. The thoughts that she can see and talk to her deceased husband
d. the suicidal thoughts

There is a myth that talking to a person about suicidal thoughts causes the person to think about or act on suicidal thoughts. For many years this was a concern for therapists.

THIS IS NOT TRUE. A person who is thinking or planning suicide will not be persuaded to act by discussing the topic of suicide. In fact, a person who is thinking about suicide may use the opportunity to be talked OUT of planning or the attempt. This is the basis of the origination of suicide hotlines. As a therapist, there is a need to constantly assess a persons suicidal thoughts and plans.

Matt is a 29 year old male that comes to you with complaints of feeling really low to a point of suicidal ideation. He has never acted on these thoughts but they occur a few times a year. This has been ongoing for 5 years. After further questioning, you learn that when he is not feeling low, he spends a lot of time on pornographic websites. This behavior has caused a divorce and Matt feels like he cannot control himself to stop. He has been watching pornography for the past 3 days and actually thought of cancelling his appointment so he could continue to watch. He can go many months without watching pornography, which includes several months before this current situation. The proper diagnosis for Matt is?

a. Bipolar Disorder, last episode manic
b. Mood Disorder with mixed features
c. Mood Disorder, Pornography Dependence
d. Major depression complicated with Divorce

Matt is experiencing symptoms associated with Bipolar Disorder. His watching of pornography and missing work would be indicated under a manic episode. He has a history of cycling behavior.

Bipolar 1 Disorder, in which the primary symptom presentation is manic, or rapid (daily) cycling episodes of mania and depression.

Emily is a 15 year old girl that complains that was referred by the school due to increase in agitation and physical aggression towards peers in school. This is not typical of the client. She has a stellar school attendance and grade report. The school informs you that her parents are going through a very messy divorce, beginning this year. You meet with Emily and give her a preliminary diagnosis of?

a. Impulse control disorder
b. Adjustment Disorder
c. Major depression
d. Intermittent Explosive Disorder

Emily is experiencing symptoms associated with Adjustment Disorder. Her behavior and grades (2 life areas) were positive before the divorce.

Adjustment Disorders: The essential feature of these disorders is the development of clinically significant emotional or behavioral symptoms in response to an identifiable psychosocial stressor(s). The clinical significance of the reaction is indicated by either marked distress that is beyond that which is expected or by impairment in social or occupations functioning.

When you have an adjustment disorder, the symptoms must appear within 3 months of the stressful event. Any type of stress can trigger an adjustment disorder, such as:

- Divorce or other relationship break-up

- An accident

- A significant loss (including the death of a loved one)

- A serious medical diagnosis

- Any major life transition or change (e.g. marriage, having a baby, retirement, changing schools, or starting a new job)

- Living through or being impacted by a disaster, such as a flood or tornado

Sometimes an adjustment disorder develops due to a combination or series of stressors, or an ongoing stressor.

Typically, the symptoms of an adjustment disorder subside within 6 months after the stressful event occurred (acute), or after any consequences of the stressor (e.g. the effects of an illness or injury) have subsided. The exception to this is when the stressor

Eddie is a 15 year old male with a past history of ADHD. He was on medication to control symptoms for 5 years, but recently came off medication. His parents express concern that he is becoming violent, verbally and physically, his grades heave dropped since coming off the medication and they feel like they cannot control him. You meet with Eddie and see he is having a hard time focusing, staying on task and is fidgeting in your entire session. What should be your first recommendation?

a.   Get consent to talk to the school to confirm parents' reports
b.   Ask Eddie how he feels about being on medication and if he would consider going back to his medication regimen
c.   Request a medical evaluation
d.   Request a psychiatric evaluation

You are in the middle of an initial outpatient session with a 40 year old mother of 2. When you ask about history of suicidal ideation, your client discloses that she thought about committing suicide yesterday. She had a very realistic plan but did not complete because she felt guilty about the effects on her children. She is very remorseful and denies any current thoughts. What should you do next?

a. Develop a safety plan with her husband
b. Complete a risk assessment and develop a safety plan
c. Call the attending psychiatrist for an immediate evaluation
d. Immediately call for assistance, including 911

The client is currently denying any suicidal ideation or intent. She also reports feelings of remorse. You should question further and complete a risk assessment to identify what her thoughts were, how often they have occurred and what her plan had been. A risk assessment will help to identify all of these factors. In addition, a safety plan often helps a client to feel accountable and to know how to reach out and to whom when this occurs.

Types of Therapy

There are several types of therapies a person can participate in, which are:

Individual: Therapy that occurs with the therapist and the patient alone.

Group: Therapy that involves the therapist and two or more clients at the same.

Marital/couples: Therapy that has a therapist and either both spouses or significant others.

Family: Therapy with the therapist and either a child and parent/guardian or children and parent(s)/guardian (s).

Support groups: Not run by a therapist. Peer run support group, where persons with a similar issue meet together at a certain place and time to support each other through the crisis or issue. Examples are 12 step programs or grief and loss group.

Peer to Peer Counseling: Peer to Peer Counseling relies on nonprofessionals assisting others who share the same issues. Peer to Peer counseling is most often used with kids or adolescents in school or therapeutic schools or residential settings.

Play Therapy: Can be used with adults, but mostly with kids or clients with autism. This approach uses items such as puppets, dolls, doll houses, and games to work with the client on expression.

Art therapy: Uses expressive arts such as painting, drawing, sculpting to help a person express their emotions and thoughts through forms and not words. utilizes a person's creative faculties in the area of art to develop their physical and emotional health. Art therapy assists in increasing well-being. It is also often used for those who are young or have difficulty with expressive language (autism).

Music Therapy: Uses sound or use of instruments to promote a sense of self-awareness, feeling of over-all well-being and ability to express themselves.

Approaches to Therapy

Psychoanalysis: Developed by Freud, this approach uses analysis of word association, dream interpretation and fantasy interpretation. The process of psychoanalysis seeks to identify how the mind and its though processes effect behavior.

Behavioral Therapy: Therapy that focuses on changing behavior through classical conditioning and operant conditioning.

Cognitive Behavioral(CBT): Approach that focuses on teaching a person how to identify their thinking errors and replace them with positive thinking. This change will produce an improved outcome (consequence) and thus alter a person's mood positively.

Person Centered (Rogerian): This approach is non-directive, and often uses reflection from the therapist to assist the person in increasing awareness and to promote self-actualization.

Dialectical behavior therapy (DBT): Approach most associated for treatment for persons with Borderline Personality Disorder. Approach teaches 4 core skills to help a person to obtain emotional regulation.

Humanistic therapy: Therapeutic approach that looks at the uniqueness and positive attributes of an individual.

Adlerian: The focus is to assist a person in adapting their feelings of inferiority. Adlerian theory believes that a persons behavioral patterns and beliefs stem from their childhood.

Solution Focused Brief Therapy: Therapy is based on client's personal current goals versus past issues. Past is referenced when there has been a history of success. The goal is future focused.

Mindfulness: This approach uses a combination of techniques to assist the person in releasing the psychological anxiety or negative feeling and to be in the moment. Techniques uses are breathing, meditation and yoga movements. Mindfulness is used with other therapies such as cognitive therapy, (MBCT), mindfulness-based stress reductions (MBSR) and most often in dialectical behavior therapy (DBT).

.Difference between rehabilitation and habilitation:

There is a difference when working with a person with a developmental disability versus working with a person mental illness

DD (developmental disabilities): Habilitation: to allow a person to function at their personal level

MI: (mentally ill) Rehabilitation: to return a person to their highest functioning level prior to a mental health break/issue/episode.

For DD- we think in terms of long term, DD is forever

For MI- we think in terms of short term, belief that people can recover

Content	DD	MH
Philosophy	Person centered	Recovery model
Role of DX	De-emphasized	Medically necessary
Assessment	Holistic and largely non clinical	Primarily clinical
Treatment	deals with ecology-the relations between living organisms and their environment	Evidence based tx of symptoms

Different words same meaning:

- Individual Plan vs treatment plan

- Outcomes vs completion

- Recovery vs completion of a goal

- Stength based vs client focused

Career Counseling

Career Development is a "continuous lifelong process of developmental experiences that focuses on seeking, obtaining and processing information about self, occupational and educational alternatives, life styles and role options" (Hansen, 1976).

Career development theory comes from the following four disciplines and fall into 4 categories:

- Differential Psychology- interest in occupation options- Trait factor (Frank Parsons)
- Personality- individual characteristics (Holland)
- Sociology- occupational goals on movement lateral or upward (Bandura)
- Developmental Psychology- where a person is at developmentally effects their current and future goals (Super)

Holland

Holland believed that career choice is based on a person's behavioral or personality style. He believed that the choice of an occupation is an expression of an individual's personality. He believed that persons in a particular occupation share similar personalities. These people have similar personalities, so their responses will be similar. He also believed that happiness in a job is when a person experiences a fit between personality and job environment.

6 Holland Types of job personalities

Realistic - this person likes to work with their hands, are active, like to use machines or tools

High traits - practical, masculine, stable; Low traits - sensitive, feminine, stable

Examples of jobs: construction worker, architecture, agriculture or farming, truck driving, or a mail carrier

Investigative – this person is very analytical, like to explore, not necessarily social
High traits – scholarly, intellectual, critical; Low traits – powerful, ambitious, adventurous

Examples of jobs: dentist, biologist, IT, chemist

Artistic -this person is interested in music, literature, emotional or creative arts

High traits – expressive, creative, spontaneous; Low traits – orderly, efficient, conventional, social, masculine

 Examples of jobs: writer, journalist, artist, musician, or poet

Social – this person is interested in educating, helping fields, human or social services High traits – cooperative, friendly, humanistic; Low traits – ambitious, creative, strong,

Examples of jobs: Therapists, social workers, nurses, CAN, police officers

Enterprising – This person is highly verbally skilled, a natural leader, very persuasive

High traits – ambitious, adventurous, energetic; Low traits – intellectual, creative, feminine

Example of jobs: CEO, executive director, lawyer, judge, politician

Conventional – This person likes to have rules and routines both personally and professionally, they have a respect for power and status

High traits – stable, efficient, dependable, controlled; Low traits – intellectual, adventurous, creative

Example of jobs: Accountant, bank clerk, tax preparer

Holland Types are usually expressed in 3 letters- Ex: RIA

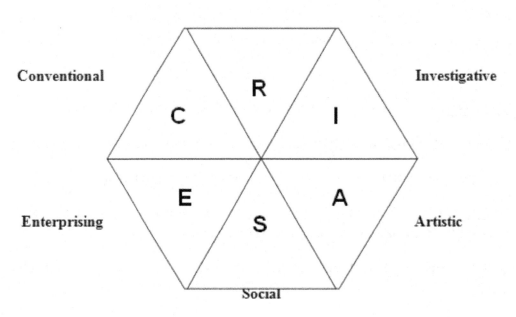

Most Masculine Types -- R & E	Most Prestigious Types -- I & E
Most Feminine Types -- A & S	Least Prestigious Types --R & C

Bandura

Career Development uses Bandura social learning theory.

It focuses on 4 areas:

- Performance Accomplishments
- Vicarious Learning
- Social Persuasion
- Physiological States and Affective Reactions

Another way to think of the theory is that our past influence our career goals. Our physical, cultural and personality all interact to influence our perceptions of who we are, what we want to do, and what we can be successful at doing.

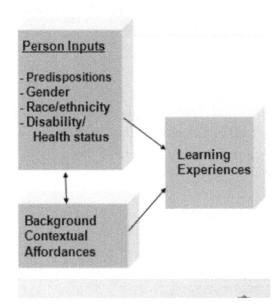

Bandura's theory also has what is known as Triadic Reciprocal Model of Causality

They are: personal attributes, external environmental factors; overt behavior

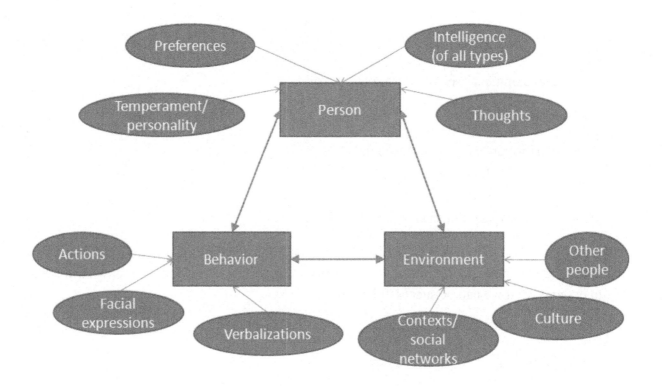

The idea is that a person is effected by their environment and past. This plays out in our career choice and happiness in our career. According to Bandura, this is how one obtains self-efficacy. People are able to take on a task or even a position if they believe they can successful.

Super's Developmental Self-Concept Theory

According to Super, vocational development is the process of developing a self-perception over time. As this becomes more real, a person's vocational choice is clearer and becomes more achievable. Work satisfaction is highly correlated with how a person has used this self perception in their work environment.

Super developed stages of career development:

Growth (Birth to mid teens) – Task: develop self-perception: shift from play to work orientation.

Fantasy (4-10 years old) - career fantasies

Interest (11-12 years old) - identifies personal interests as a basis for career choices

Capacity (13-14 years old) – becomes more focused on skills that meet requirements of jobs.

Exploration (Mid teens through early 20's) - Task: to develop and implement self perception through trails at different jobs. Begin to develop preferences in roles.

Tentative (15-17 years old) – trials at part time jobs, volunteer work or classes in career field.

Crystallization of Preference (18-21 years old) – Choosing a college or career path

Establishment (mid 20's through mid 40's) – Task: to find a secure a field of choice/ professional preference

Trial and Stabilization (25-30 years old) - May make a few moves during this time, but attempting to find the right job to stabilize

Advancement (30-40 years old) – continued effort to remain in the job or set up for promotions

Maintenance (40's through early 60's) - Task is to preserve one's position in the company or the field. Little to no change may occur in career path or in company.

Disengagement or Decline (Late 60's through retirement) – Task: Decrease in activity at work and preparation to decrease time in workforce or to retire.

LIFE RAINBOW

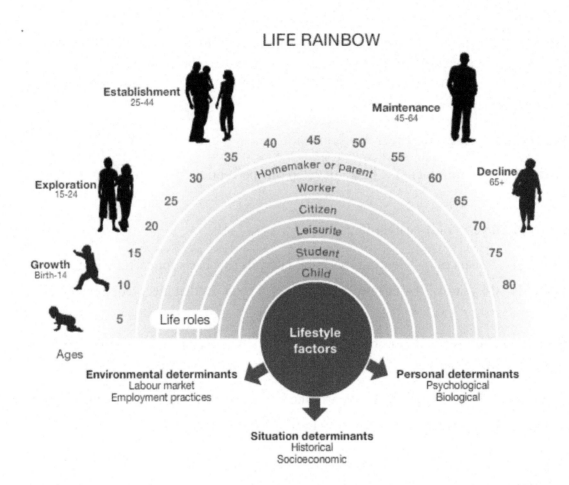

Establishment
25-44

Maintenance
45-64

Exploration
15-24

Decline
65+

Growth
Birth-14

40   45   50

35   55

30   Homemaker or parent   60

25   Worker   65

20   Citizen   70

15   Leisurite   75

Child   80

10

5   Student

Life roles

Ages

Lifestyle
factors

Environmental determinants
Labour market
Employment practices

Personal determinants
Psychological
Biological

Situation determinants
Historical
Socioeconomic

76

PARSON'S THEORY OF CAREER DEVELOPMENT

Parson's developed the Trait and factor theory used for career development counselling. According to Parson's, a person will perform at their best if their career fits both their personality and abilities. In his book, 'Choosing a Vocation', Parsons maintains that personal counsel is fundamental to the career search. In particular, he notes seven stages for a career counsellor to work through with clients:

1. Personal data: to gather key facts about the person, including facts of what is obstructing career goal
2. Self-analysis: a thorough analysis of a person's interests and other potential issues that might impact on the choice of career.
3. The client's own choice and decision: this should be stated or created by the client
4. Counsellor's analysis: the counsellor gives input and may use assessments to ensure the clients choices are a good fit.
5. Outlook on the vocational field: counsellor analyzes and discusses industries in the field, their current status and future outlook
6. Induction and advice: reasonable and objective
7. General helpfulness: the counsellor assists client in moving in the direction of career

Krumboltz's Learning Theory of Career Counseling (LTCC)

Krumboltz model is based on social learning model and emphasizes the importance of learning experiences and their effect on occupational selection. Krumboltz believed that an individual's unique learning experiences over their life is what influences career choice. These influences are:

- The overview of one's self that comes from meeting learned standard in one's experiences and performance.
- The ability to use developed skills to cope with the environment.
- Career-entry behavior such as applying for a job or selecting an educational or training institution.
- Career decision making is an important skill that is used throughout one's career.
- An individual's preference come from multiple factors that include cognitive processes, influences from the environment, and one's own individualized inherited personal characteristics and traits.

This theory believes that both negative and positive experiences impact a person's career beliefs. In addition, unpredictable social and environmental conditions also have an influence. Because of these influences, the career counselor should focus on 5 skills:

- Curiosity
- Persistence
- Flexibility
- Optimism
- Risk-taking

John Krumboltz   **LEARNING THEORY**

- Positive Reinforcement - a positive experience leads to learning and acquiring more skills related to that experience
- Negative Reinforcement – a negative experience leads to avoiding activities related to that experience
- Positive Role Models – influence career decisions based on positive expectations for self
- Self Efficacy – a strong belief in own abilities lead to expectations of positive expectations of self in imagined career-related activities

---

Tiedeman Decision Making Theory for Career

Tiedeman's theory of decision-making theory for career development believes that a person is accountable for one's own choice and behavior. Tiedeman, believes that when a person view the a situation as possibly having a negative outcome, it has an impact on their decision to engage in behavior. In terms of career, if a person believes they may fail, they will not try. In contrast, if a person believes they can be successful, they will often attempt. Tiedeman believed there were 7 stages in decision making:

- Exploration
- Crystallization
- Choice
- Clarification
- Induction
- Reformation
- Integration

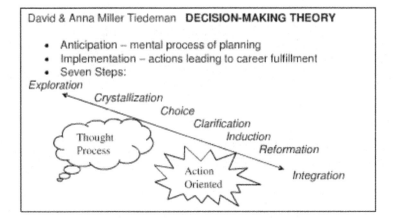

Reardon Cognitive Information Processing

A newer theory developed in 2003 by Reardon et al, this theory was focused on using theory and placing it into practice in a cost effective approach. They believed that career choice and counseling practices should be based on Problem solving and decision-making. There are 5 steps (CASEV):

Communication

- External demands: Event, Significant other: What is impacting us at the time
- Internal affective, behavioral, or physiological states: Emotions, Avoidance Behavior, Physiological: How we think or feel both physically and emotionally

Analysis

- Enhance self-knowledge: Having an understanding of one's Values, Interests, Skills, and Employment preferences
- Enhance occupational knowledge: learning about the requirements and expectations of a career or job.
- Generic information processing skills: Self-talk, Self-awareness, Control and monitoring

Synthesis

- Elaboration: looking at all alternative options
- Crystallization: A more focused list of potential options

Valuing: Outweighing the benefits and costs to each potential Opportunity

Execution: Develop a plan; Prep for education or training, application, interview

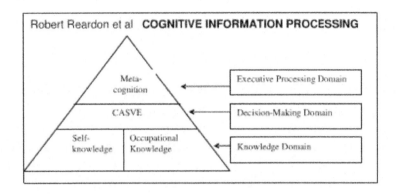

Robert Reardon et al **COGNITIVE INFORMATION PROCESSING**

- Meta-cognition ← Executive Processing Domain
- CASVE ← Decision-Making Domain
- Self-knowledge / Occupational Knowledge ← Knowledge Domain

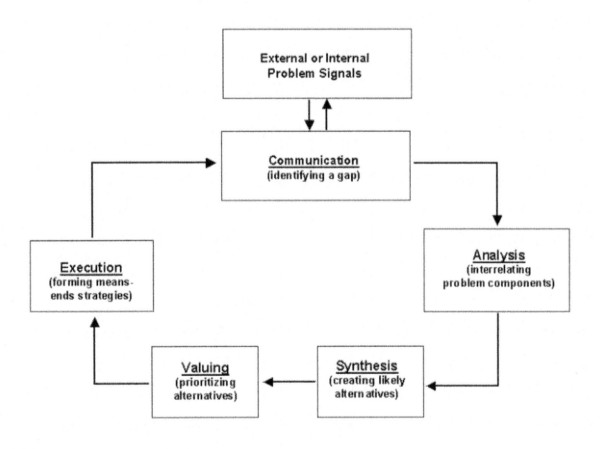

External or Internal Problem Signals

Communication
(identifying a gap)

Analysis
(interrelating problem components)

Synthesis
(creating likely alternatives)

Valuing
(prioritizing alternatives)

Execution
(forming means-ends strategies)

Statistics and Psychology

Statistics are used to Organize Data, Describe Data and Make Inferences Based on the Data. Many students become anxious when they learn they need to take statistics for a psychology degree. But there was a need for it. In psychology there are many ways a counselor analyzes many variables relating to a human. A counselor will have to use statistics when using psychological testing, career testing, risk assessments, and other tools such as an ICAP or Mortimer-Filkens test for substance use patterns, as well as in ISP's for persons with developmental disabilities and even in treatment planning for mental health. These are the key terms in statistics in psychology:

Alternative Hypothesis: This states that the independent variable has a direct effect on the independent variable and that chance is not involved.

Case-study: Use of a single individual to relate the condition or treatment progress or lack of progress.

Control Group: Research of a group of subjects that is treated as the experimental group but does not actually receive any treatment.

Correlational design: Patterns of correlations are analyzed in this design.

Dependent Variable: Variable designated to measure the effect of the independent variable.

Descriptive Statistics: Data presented in numerical form. Examples are: mean, median, mode.

External Validity: How data results transform from specific subjects to the larger population.

F-ratio: A statistical index relating systematic variation in the data (caused by treatment effects plus random error) to unsystematic variability in the data (caused by random error alone). The effects of treatments plus error is the numerator and the effect of error (chance) is the denominator of the F-ratio

Independent Variable: In research, the variable that is manipulated to identify a result.

Inferential Statistics: Data is used to make inferences about population characteristics through the process of hypothesis testing.

Longitudinal Study: Research of a group over an extended period of time

Matched-Subjects Designs: Subjects are matched on one or more similar variables or characteristics to reduce between groups variability.

Mean: A measure of central tendency in an average set of scores: Average

Median: Measure of central tendency, which gives value of the middlemost score: Middle value

Mode: Value that occurs the most often in a set of scores.

Naturalistic Observation: Recording of the behavior that is occurring naturally without the observer effecting the pattern or behavior.

Nominal scale: Data is sorted into different categories.

Null hypothesis: belief that the independent variable will not effect the dependent variable and if an effect occurs, it was by chance.

Observational Research: The systematic study of behavior of a subject or subjects, as it occurs in the environment.

Ordinal scale: A scale of measurement where data are put in order, but where there is no fixed amount of difference between the points on the scale.

Placebo effect: A positive result when no treatment was received. Subject in the control group.

Random sampling: Subjects are selected randomly or in lottery style.

Reliability: The consistency with which a measuring instrument is consistent (

Significance: Low probability that the results occurred by chance, and would be more likely attributed to the treatment.

Significance Level: Type I Error: when the null hypothesis is correct, but rejected.

Standard Deviation: Calculated from the square root of the variance in order to give a value in the same range as raw scores. The standard deviation is the spread of scores around the mean of the sample.

Standard Error: The standard deviation of the sampling distribution of the mean of one sample.

Type I Error: when the null hypothesis is correct, but rejected

Type II Error: When the null hypothesis is retained when it is not true.

Validity: The statistical instrument measures what it is designated to measure.

Variable: A property that can take different values or that can be

Z-score: Standard score: units of standard deviations from the mean.

There are three essential components of the scientific method for psychological statistics: Design, measurement, and analysis. Design is very important as if the design is not solid, the data will be skewed. The hypothesis must be well designed and the variables independent and dependent identified. Once established, it is important to identify a valid measuring tool.

Types of Psychological Tests

Intelligence Assessments: Intelligence tests measure a person's general level of intelligence. The most common intelligence tests are: Standford-Binet and Wechsler scales.

Stanford-Binet

Wechsler scales: Wechsler Adult Intelligence Scale—Fourth Edition (WAIS-IV) is used for those 16 and older. Children under 16, receive the Wechsler Intelligence Scale for Children Fourth Edition (WISC-IV).

The WAIS-IV is categorized into four scales to derive a full scale IQ. Each scale has multiple subscales.

Verbal Comprehension Scale

- Similarities
- Vocabulary
- Information
- Supplemental Subtest: Comprehension

Perceptual Reasoning Scale

- Block Design
- Matrix Reasoning
- Visual Puzzles
- Supplemental Subtests: Picture Completion; Figure Weights (16-69) only

Working Memory Scale

- Digit Span
- Arithmetic
- Supplemental Subtest: Letter-Number Sequencing (16-69 only)

Processing Speed Scale

- Symbol Search
- Coding
- Supplemental Subtest: Cancellation (16-69 only)

IQ Range ("deviation IQ")	IQ Classification
130 and above	Very Superior
120–129	Superior
110–119	High Average
90–109	Average
80–89	Low Average
70–79	Borderline
69 and below	Extremely Low

Personality Assessments: Personality assessment help counselors to better understand the client. There are twotypes of personality tests : Objective and Subjective.

Objective test: Minnesota Multiphasic Personality Inventory (MMPI-2)

Projective tests: Rorschach Inkblot Test and the Thematic Apperception Test (TAT)

The MMPI-2 is not meant for healthy personalities. It measures for personality traits that are dysfunctional such as: paranoia, mania, social ineptness, masculinity/femininity, and other psychopathology traits. There are over 50 questions on this test. There are also validity scales to help determine if a person is trying to manipulate the outcome of the test results.

Number	Abbreviation	Description	What is measured	No. of items
1	Hs	Hypochondriasis	Concern with bodily symptoms	32
2	D	Depression	Depressive Symptoms	57
3	Hy	Hysteria	Awareness of problems and vulnerabilities	60
4	Pd	Psychopathic Deviate	Conflict, struggle, anger, respect for society's rules	50
5	MF	Masculinity/Femininity	Stereotypical masculine or feminine interests/behaviors	56
6	Pa	Paranoia	Level of trust, suspiciousness, sensitivity	40
7	Pt	Psychasthenia	Worry, Anxiety, tension, doubts, obsessiveness	48
8	Sc	Schizophrenia	Odd thinking and social alienation	78
9	Ma	Hypomania	Level of excitability	46
0	Si	Social Introversion	People orientation	69

Abbreviation	New in version	Description	Assesses
CNS	1	"Cannot Say"	Questions not answered
L	1	Lie	Client "faking good"
F	1	Infrequency	Client "faking bad" (in first half of test)
K	1	Defensiveness	Denial/Evasiveness
Fb	2	Back F	Client "faking bad" (in last half of test)
VRIN	2	Variable Response Inconsistency	answering similar/opposite question pairs inconsistently
TRIN	2	True Response Inconsistency	answering questions all true/all false
F-K	2	F minus K	honesty of test responses/not faking good or bad
S	2	Superlative Self-Presentation	improving upon K scale, "appearing excessively good"
Fp	2	F-Psychopathology	Frequency of presentation in clinical setting
Fs	2-RF	Infrequent Somatic Response	Overreporting of somatic symptoms

These are the factors (A-O and Q1-Q4) evaluated in the test:

A. Warmth
B. Reasoning
C. Emotional Stability
D. Dominance
E. Liveliness
F. Rule-Consciousness
G. Social Boldness
H. Sensitivity
I. Vigilance
J. Abstractedness
K. Privateness
L. Apprehension
M. Openness to Change
N. Self-Reliance
O. Perfectionism
P. Tension

Projective tests: Rorschach Inkblot Test and the Thematic Apperception Test (TAT)

Projective test take a person's interpretation and then compare it to the normal and abnormal response and score the response. There are only 10 cards in the test. 5 black and white and 5 colored.   Each test response is then compared to the norm response. Here is a Rorschach card.

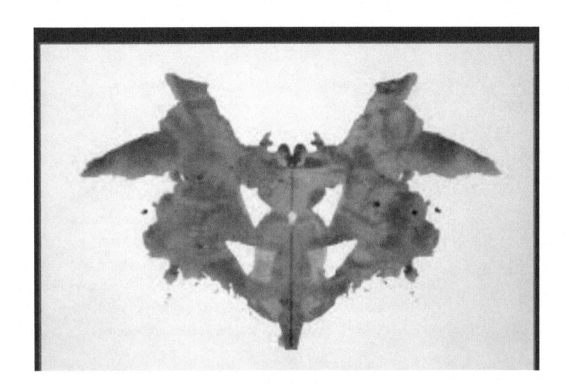

Thematic Apperception Test (TAT)

The Thematic Apperception Test (TAT) has 31 cards that a subject has to describe what they think the story is behind the picture. This test is not formally scored, but rather it is written how the subject interprets the scene. There is no right or wrong answer. It is meant to solicit a persons thinking or thought process. An example of a picture from the TAT.

Practice Test Questions

1. Freud is best known for his theory on personality. He had 5 stages of development. Which is the correct sequence?
    a.   Oral, anal, phallic, latency, genital
    b.   Anal, phallic, genital, latency, oral
    c.   Latency, genital, anal, oral, phallic
    d.   Oral, genital, phallic, latency, anal

2. Jean Piaget is best known for his theory of cognitive development. What are Piaget's stages of development?
    a.   Oral, anal, phallic, latency, genital
    b.   Sensorimotor stage , preoperational stage , concrete operational stage , formal operational stage
    c.   Intimacy vs isolation, generativity vs stagnation
    d.   Preconventional, conventional, postconventional

3. Behavioral theory is based on the concept that all human beings learn a new behavior by being conditioned to the behavior. Who are 2 famous behaviorists?
    a.   Freud and Kohlberg
    b.   Erickson and Horney
    c.   Skinner and Watson
    d.   Maslow and Freud

4. Erik Erickson was influenced by Freud's theory of personality. While there are some similarities there is a very large difference. Which statement best describes the difference between the 2 theorists.
    a. Erikson focused on conflicts that take place within the ego versus Freud who focused on the conflict between the id and ego.
    b. Erickson focused on the conflict between the ego and superego where Freud focused on the conflict between the id and ego.
    c. Erickson did not believe there was any internal conflict and Freud believed all conflict to be internal
    d.   Erickson believed that conflicts were always resolved and Freud believed that most conflicts were unresolved.

5. Erik Erickson developed the stages of psychosocial development. Erickson believed that people experience a crisis in these stages. Resolved crisis leads to a healthy personality and strong virtues. What stage takes place in the adolescent years?

    a. Intimacy vs isolation
    b. identity vs role confusion
    c. generativity vs stagnation
    d identity vs intimacy

6. What is the counseling technique used when a counselor purposely upsets a client in order to provoke an intensified response in order for the client to understand their irrational response?

    a. Confrontation
    b. Paradoxical Intention
    c. Shaping
    d Extinction

7. Most states are concerned with medication reduction plans. You have a client that the psychiatrist reports are in medical therapeutic range. The client's behaviors have significantly decreased and is responding well and progresing. What is the first step you should do?

    a. Talk to the client about reducing medication
    b. Talk to the psychiatrist and receive a report on the benefits of remaining on the medication.
    c. Tell the client he needs to talk to his doctor
    d. Suggest that the client should begin a slow process of coming off his medication with a regimented schedule of reduction

8. Bandura created a social learning theory. He believed that there was a social element to learning, which included that people learn behaviors by watching other people interact. This is known as:

    a. Modeling
    b. Shaping
    c. Social conformity
    d. Conditioning

9. Bandura social learning theory indicated that not all behavior is through observation. There are also other ways to learn behavior. What statement best describes his theory?

    a. attention, shaping, conditioning, conformity
    b. attention, retention, social conformity, conditioning
    c. attention, retention, reproduction, motivation
    d. attention, conformity, shaping, motivation

10. Group therapy is highly efficient for many people. Groups often have a purpose. Some groups are more open or process, while other group seek a specified outcome, change or topic. Which of the following groups are more outcome or goal driven?

    a. Process group
    b. 12 step group
    c. Art therapy group
    d. Behavioral group

11. Group Therapy that is best suited for people who wish to discuss their issues in a manner to resolve the issues are:

    a. Process group
    b. Employment readiness group
    c. Art therapy group
    d. Behavioral group

12. A 6 month old child begins to cry whenever separated from itsw mother. This behavior is consistent with which theory?

    a. Personality Theory
    b. Behavioral theory
    c. Attachment Theory
    d. Abnormal Psychology Theory

13. Suzi is a client that continues to voice concern that she feels she wants a man to become close to her but struggles when they do. She has described several incidents where she has become very overwhelmed and acted in ways that actually push men away. This behavior has been a pattern for many years. This pattern of intense behavior has called her to call off 2 engagements and 1 engagement to be called off by a potential spouse. What is a possible initial diagnosis?

    a. Mood Disorder
    b. Bipolar disorder
    c. Social Phobia
    d. Borderline Personality Disorder

14. Joey has an intellectual disability. His FSIQ is 40. He often becomes physically aggressive whenever there is any change. A staff has resigned after 10 years of working with him. What would be the proper protocol for helping Joey to adjust to the change?

    a. Tell Joey the day of the change in staff
    b. Have the new staff be introduced by his current staff for a few days before to help with the transition
    c. Have the current staff tell Joey everyday that she is leaving to help him acclimate
    d. Don't tell Joey information because it may upset him, but tell his parents so they are aware

15. You have a client that comes to you because their spouse of 20 years has passed away 2 months ago. She complains of feeling sad, cries often, has difficulty completing tasks and has trouble going to work and has called in 10 times during the past 2 months. The proper diagnosis at this time is?

    a. Major Depression
    b. Adjustment Disorder
    c. Psychosis
    d. Mood Disorder NOS

16. You have a client that comes to you because their spouse of 20 years has passed away 1 year ago. She complains of feeling depressed, cries all the time, feels like she can talk to him and see him, has difficulty completing tasks and has trouble going to work and has called in 10 times during the past 2 months. And often thinks of suicide. The proper diagnosis at this time is?

    a. Major Depression
    b. Adjustment Disorder
    c. Psychosis
    d. Major Depression with Suicidal features

17. Amanda is a 22 year old client with a history of legal involvement for marijuana. She used marijuana daily and also distributed marijuana. Amanda has begun drinking at lease a 6 pack almost daily. She also now has a DUI. She has not used or sold marijuana in over a year. What is her diagnosis?

    a. Marijuana Abuse, Alcohol Abuse
    b. Alcohol abuse
    c. Alcohol Dependent
    d. Alcohol Dependent, Marijuana Abuse

18. Matt is a 29 year old male that comes to you with complaints of feeling really low to a point of suicidal ideation. He has never acted on these thoughts but they occur a few times a year. This has been ongoing for 5 years. After further questioning, you learn that when he is not feeling low, he spends a lot of time on pornographic websites. This behavior has caused a divorce and Matt feels like he cannot control himself to stop. He has been watching pornography for the past 3 days and actually thought of cancelling his appointment so he could continue to watch. He can go many months without watching pornography, which includes several months before this current situation. The proper diagnosis for Matt is?

    a. Bipolar Disorder, last episode manic
    b. Mood Disorder with mixed features
    c. Mood Disorder, Pornography Dependence
    d. Major depression complicated with Divorce

19. Emily is a 15 year old girl that complains that was referred by the school due to increase in agitation and physical aggression towards peers in school. This is not typical of the client. She has a stellar school attendance and grade report. The school informs you that her parents are going through a very messy divorce, beginning this year. You meet with Emily and give her a preliminary diagnosis of?

    a. Impulse control disorder
    b. Adjustment Disorder
    c. Major depression
    d. Intermittent Explosive Disorder

20. Eddie is a 15 year old male with a past history of ADHD. He was on medication to control symptoms for 5 years, but recently came off medication. His parents express concern that he is becoming violent, verbally and physically, his grades heave dropped since coming off the medication and they feel like they cannot control him. You meet with Eddie and see he is having a hard time focusing, staying on task and is fidgeting in your entire session. What should be your first recommendation?

    a. Get consent to talk to the school to confirm parents' reports
    b. Ask Eddie how he feels about being on medication and if he would consider going back to his medication regimen
    c. Request a medical evaluation
    d. Request a psychiatric evaluation

21. You are in the middle of an initial outpatient session with a 40 year old mother of 2. When you ask about history of suicidal ideation, your client discloses that they thought about committing suicide yesterday. They had a very realistic plan but did not complete because they felt guilty about the effects on her children. She is very remorseful and denies any current thoughts. What should you do next?

    a. Develop a safety plan with her husband
    b. Complete a risk assessment and develop a safety plan
    c. Call the attending psychiatrist for an immediate evaluation
    d. Immediately call for assistance, including 911

22. Career development is crucial to many clients. Who developed the theory regarding fields and levels?

    a. Roe
    b. Erickson
    c. Holland
    d. Super

23. To understand career development, the theory of career maturity was developed by what theorist?

    a. Roe
    b. Erickson
    c. Crites
    d. Super

24. A client you have been seeing for the past 3 months proposes that you meet for coffee after your session. According to what standard should you reject the offer?

    a. The ethical standards of practice
    b. The medical malpractice bylaws
    c. Your companies policy about client counselor contact
    d. all the above

25. Bobby is a 3 year old child. His father tells him to clean his toys in his room. Bobby's first response is "no". His father tells him to clean the room because, "I told you to". This form of parenting is known as?

    a. Authoritarian
    b. Permissive
    c. Enabling
    d. Pessimistic

26. As a clinician, many are fearful about asking about suicide. What is the myth about suicide?

    a. Asking about suicidal thought or plans make a person suicidal
    b. If you are suicidal and talk about it, you will act on your thoughts
    c. People who talk about suicide are seeking attention
    d. If people talk about suicide they are not serious about their intent

27. Jerry usually follows the rules at home and school because he does not want to get grounded. His behavior can be explained by what stage of Kohlberg's theory?

    a. conventional
    b. Preconventional
    c. Postconventional
    d. nonconventional

28. Karen Horney developed the most noted theory on neurosis. Horney believed that neurosis stemmed from which of the following anxiety issues?

    a. Over zealous parents, lack of clearly identified rules, indifference, erratic parental
    b. physical abuse, mental abuse, sexual abuse
    c. lack of real guidance, disparaging attitudes, too much admiration or the absence of it, lack of reliable warmth, having to take sides in parental disagreements, too much or too little responsibility, over-protection, isolation from other children
    d. all the above

29. Horney had a list of 10 neurotic needs that could be summarized into categories. These categories are?

    a. Needs that move you away, towards or against others
    b. Needs that move you towards or away from a person
    c. Needs that make you accept or reject a person
    d. Needs that make the relationship healthy or unhealthy

30. According to Horney, healthy individuals use which of the categories depending on internal and external factors?

    a. Needs that move you away,
    b. Needs that move you towards
    c. Needs that make you against
    d. all the above

31. Mindfulness Cognitive Therapy is best used for what conditions?

    a. Medical
    b. Emotional
    c. Medical and Emotional
    d. None of the above

32. Maslow developed the hierarchy of needs. What is the correct order?

    a. Physiological, security and safety, love/belonging, esteem, self-actualization
    b. Physiological, love/belonging, esteem, self-actualization, realization
    c. Physiological,longing, safety, esteem, self-actualization
    d. Safety, love/belonging, esteem, self-actualization

33. Maslow viewed the needs of security and safety to include:

    a. Financial
    b. Health
    c. Overall well-ness
    d. all the above

34. Bowlby is noted for his theory on attachment. Which is the correct statement regarding his theory?

    a. Secure, Ambivalent, Avoidant, Disorganized,
    b. Secure, Avoidant, Detached, Connected
    c. Attached, non-atttached, avoidant, solitary
    d. Attached, avoidant, secure, unavailable

35. Piaget believed that we learn about our world through schemas. A schema is a way to physically and mentally categorize information about our world. What statement best describes Piaget's theory?

    a. Assimilation, Accommodation, Individuation
    b. Assimilation
    c. Assimilation, Accommodation, equilibration
    d. Accomodation

36. Watson created a behavioral psychology theory. He believed that human beings respond to their environment based on external stimuli and not internal stimuli. He believed that all human beings can change their behavior through a process known as conditioning. What is the best statement that describes his theory?

    a. Behaviors can be changed only through operant conditioning.
    b. Behaviors can be changed through classical or operant conditioning
    c. Behaviors can be observed through classical or operant conditioing
    d. none of the above

37. The most noted behaviorists are?

    a. Watson, Skinner, Freud, Erickson
    b. Watson, Skinner, Pavlov, Thorndike
    c. Watson, Horney, Bandura, Freud
    d. all of the above

38. Maureen is in first grade and she is demonstrating difficulty playing well with her peers. Her teacher puts her on a sticker program, where she earns a sticker each day she plays well with the other students and does not earn a sticker when she has a conflict. At the end of the week she can earn a prize if she has 4 out of 5 stickers. This sticker program is an example of an application of what theory?

    a. Behavioral Theory
    b. Cognitive Behavioral Theory
    c. Social Psychology Theory
    d. Personality Theory

39. Which theory believes that our thoughts and feelings influence our behaviors and that changing the way we think about a situation will improve our behavior?

    a. Behavioral Theory
    b. Cognitive Behavioral Theory
    c. Social Psychology Theory
    d. Personality Theory

40. Mary is a 40 year old wife and mother of 2 grade school age children. Her primary complaint for entering therapy is that she has recently begun to feel overwhelmed at home and with the kids. She feels she is losing her temper quickly with her kids, but also with her spouse and friends. After assessing and concluding that Mary is not experiencing depression, what theory best address Mary's complaints?

    a. Behavioral Theory
    b. Abnormal Psychology Theory
    c. Social Psychology Theory
    d. Cognitive Behavioral Theory

41. You have a client enter his initial therapy session. Sam is a 45 year old executive director for a large company. He reports feelings of deep sadness, moments of suicidal thoughts and fears that he is going to lose everything. He often wakes up with racing thoughts and experiencing physical symptoms of racing heart and sweating. He often feels like he is dying when this occurs. As his clinician, in what order should you begin your evaluation?

    a. Suicidal ideation, medical, depressive symptoms
    b. Medical, anxiety, depression
    c. Anxiety, depression, job status
    d. Depression, Anxiety, Finances

42. Krumboltz believed in social learning theory to conduct career counseling. He believed that career choice was based on 2 factors. These 2 factors are?

    a. Cognition and Behavior
    b. Cognition and Schema
    c. Behavior and Schema
    d. None of the above

43. Cognitive distortions are thinking errors people use to justify the way they think or feel about their actions or the actions of others. There are many types of distortions. Which of the following are considered cognitive distortions?

    a. Minimizing
    b. Catastrophizing
    c. Blaming
    d. All the above

44. What theory is best suited for practice with someone who has cognitive distortions?

    a. Behavioral Theory
    b. Cognitive Behavioral Theory
    c. Social Psychology Theory
    d. Personality Theory

45. Confidentiality is important in therapy. There are times where it is necessary to break patient confidentiality. When is it necessary to break patient confidentiality?

    a. When a client is talking about an affair
    b. When a client is reporting suicidal ideation with a plan
    c. When a child of 5 years old reports getting hit with a belt and there are marks on his back
    d. B and C

46. A 60 year old woman comes to you with symptoms related to depression after the loss of her husband. According to Erickson Psychosocial stages of development which stage is she in?

    a. depression vs depression relating to complicated grief and loss
    b. Intimacy vs isolation
    c. Generativity vs Stagnation
    d. a and c

47. The cerebral cortex or the frontal lobes are responsible for

    a. emotions
    b. judgments
    c. sympathy
    d. all of the above

48. Jung created archetypes. He believed the creation of the self archetype occurs through a process known as?

    a. Intimacy
    b. Individuation
    c. individualizaion
    d. none of the above

49. Jung's belief is that the archetype of shadow is based on instincts which are the best statement?

    a. The shadow archetype is based on repressed ideas, weaknesses and desires.
    b. The shadow archetype is based on sexual desires, anger desires, and desires of violence.
    c. The shadow archetype is based on desires and weaknesses
    d. none of the above

50. According to Yalom, group therapy produces a sense of altruism. What is the best statement of how altruism is important in the process because:

    a. Group members share their strengths. This boosts self confidence and self esteem of the members.
    b. Group members share their concerns. This opens up an openness of communication.
    c. Group members can help each other through being genuine.
    d. all of the above

51. Yalom believed there were many therapeutic factors that occur during group, including altruism. He also believed that universality occurred. Which is the best statement?

    a. Universality is when a member of the group can be inspired or motivated by another member.
    b. Shared experiences and feeling promotes a sense of membership and raises self esteem.
    c. Group members can help each other through being genuine.
    d. None of the above

52. What is the definition of ethnocentrism

    a. That one person is superior over another
    b. That a person feels that they are most important.
    c. That one culture is more superior over another culture.
    d. That a person's belief system is superior to another's.

53. Festinger developed a Cognitive Dissonance Theory. According to the theory, cognitive dissonance is described as:

    a. Cognitive dissonance occurs when our behaviors do not match with our attitudes and beliefs.
    b. Cognitive dissonance is our need to keep our attitudes and beliefs in harmony.
    c. When cognitive dissonance leaves a feeling of discomfort..
    d. All the above.

54. What theorist work is most often used by therapists to understand race and cultures?

    a.   Freud
    b.   Rogers
    c.   Skinner
    d.   Watson

55. What statement best describes the concept of therapeutic surrender?

    a.   When a client fails in treatment
    b.   When a client reports surrendering to their addictions
    c.   When a client has build rapport with the therapist and begins to openly express based on trust
    d.   When a client struggles to build a trusting relationship with the therapist

56. What statement best describes the definition of transference?

    a.   Unconscious placement of feelings onto a person based on feelings one has from someone else in their life.
    b.   Conscious decision to direct onto a person based on feelings one has from someone else in their life
    c.   Subconscious redirection of feelings onto a person based on feelings one has from someone else in their life
    d.   none of the above

57. The therapist's role in person centered therapy is to

    a.   Use genuiness
    b.   Use empathy
    c.   To be non- judgemental
    d.   all of the above

58. When a client experience transference towards a therapist, the feelings a client can have can be

    a.   Negative only
    b.   Positive or Negative
    c.   Positive only
    d.   Neither positive or negative

59. Mark and Denise are a married couple for the past 15 years. They come to you to work on their marriage. They both report continued arguments and inability to get along. Mark wants to make marriage work, but Denise is strongly considering divorce. Denise says the only reasons she is agreeing to therapy is for the kids. As their therapist, what should you include as part of their preliminary treatment plan?

    a.   Weekly couples sessions with both clients
    b.   Individual sessions with each as needed
    c.   Homework to be done each week
    d.   All of the above

60. Mindfulness Cognitive Therapy is best used for what conditions?

   a.   Medical
   b.   Emotional
   c.   Medical and Emotional
   d.   None of the above

61. Cognitive behavioral theory is based on the concept that you think, you feel, and then you do. Cognitive Behavioral Theory uses "ABC's" . What are the ABC's?

   a.   Activating event, beliefs, consequences
   b.   Actions, beliefs, consequences
   c.   Activating event, behaviors, consequences
   d.   Activating event, behaviors, conflict

62. Jessica is a 35 year old woman who enters into treatment with complaints of being addicted to prescription painkillers for the past 2 years. She is now up to 3000mg per day. In your initial session you find out that she has had 5 pregnancies and has 4 children. When discussing the loss of one of the pregnancies, Jessica begins to cry. The loss of the pregnancy was 3 years ago and then she became pregnant quickly after. Her youngest child has significant disabilities. Jessica reported she began to use pain killers after the birth of her last child. Given this information, what is a potential diagnosis?

   a.   Post Partum Depression
   b.   Major Depression
   c.   Major Depression with Post partum onset
   d.   Major Depression induced by substance dependence

63. Mark is a 8 year old client. His mother initiates counseling after her son received poor grades in his first semester. Last year, the teacher reported some issues with following directions and getting into trouble during recess, his grades were average to poor. This year the teacher has the same concern, as well as concerns that Mark has difficulty staying on task and often gets up during the class and moves around. Mark's mother reports she has trouble at home with impulsivity and difficulty sitting still. What is a possible diagnosis?

   a.   Attention Deficit, hyper activity disorder (ADHD)
   b.   Attention Deficit Disorder (ADD)
   c.   Impulse Control Disorder
   d.   Not enough information to make a diagnosis

64. Morality, problem solving, acceptance of facts, non judgmental responses and creativity are all part of what level of Maslow's hierarchy of needs?

   a.   Esteem
   b.   Safety
   c.   Physiological
   d.   Self-actualization

65. Which of the following are considered projective tests?

   a.   Rorschach
   b.   (TAT) Thematic Apperception Test
   c.   WISC III
   d.   both a and b

66. A client that you have been seeing for over a year has a diagnosis of major depression and often has suicidal thoughts. Your client has not shared with anyone that she is in counseling. You get a call from your client that she is suicidal and has a plan. Her plan is viable and she has the means to engage her plan. You know she is not at home, but she has not told you where she is located. She hangs up the phone and will not respond to your calls. You do not have enough information to give to the police, yet you know she is in trouble. In your initial session, you did have her sign an agreement and consent to contact her husband if she is in crisis. Should you call the husband to inform him of the situation?

    a.   Yes, because confidentiality is not an issue when someone is in imminent danger.

    b.   Yes, because her husband should know the information.

    c.   No, because you would be breaking her confidentiality.

    d.   No, because you should call a crisis line first.

67. It is the holidays and your client gives you a small gift of under $10. Is it ethical to accept the present?

    a.   No, because it would jeopardize your therapeutic relationship

    b.   Yes, because you do not want to offend your client.

    c.   Maybe, depending on the monetary value, possible cultural issues relating to how the client will respond to accepting or rejecting the gift, and the client's motivation in giving you the gift.

    d.   No, it is completely unethical.

68. You have a 7 year old client that was referred by the school due to aggressive behaviors toward the other students. Your client seemed very agitated at the beginning of the session. The client reports problems at home with his dad. He stated that he got in trouble for fighting and his father hit him with a belt on his back. You ask the client to show you his back. You clearly see many marks that would be consistent with getting hit with a belt. The client says he is often hit by his dad with a belt but he never told anyone. As a mandated reporter, what do you need to do?

    a.   Call the client's mom to confirm the story

    b.   Call the department of family services to report abuse.

    c.   Send the client home and make sure you document the information

    d.   none of the above

69. You begin to see a 5 year old for grief counseling after her mother passed away. What type of therapy would be most appropriate?

    a. Play therapy
    b. Behavioral therapy
    c. Cognitive-Behavioral therapy
    d. Person-centered therapy

70. Experiential therapy allows a person to work through conscious or unconscious issues through alternative therapeutic technique or therapies. Examples of experiential therapy includes:

    a. Recreational therapy
    b. Equine therapy
    c. Art therapy
    d. All the above

71. Clinical supervision is a key variable for training, new or even seasoned clinicians. Clinical supervision provides many benefits. Which statement is the most accurate way to describe the benefits of supervision?

    a. Supervision helps to ensure that the clinician is managing their paperwork/
    b. Supervision helps to ensure that the clinician is continuing to work towards professional growth and development of skills.
    c. To ensure that the client is receiving quality care.
    d. Both B and C

72. A new counselor begins a new job in a very small private practice. The counselor is nervous that she will not receive clinical supervision. What are her options?

    a. She can hire a clinical supervisor not associated with the practice
    b. She can go without supervision, she is recently trained at her school, so it should be ok for a year.
    c. She should wait to see if the practice offers supervision
    d. She can talk with her past teachers for advice on her cases.

73. As part of your initial assessment, you always complete a mental status exam. What statement best describes the goals of the mental status exam?

    a.   To determine if the person is psychotic
    b.   To determine if the person is oriented to time, person and place
    c.   To determine if the person needs crisis intervention
    d.   To determine the diagnosis

74. A 22 year old client comes in for her first session. She describes her symptoms as drinking to excess, having difficulty completing tasks and also she has times of being preoccupied or lack motivation. At times she will overspend on "as seen on tv products", sometimes $1000/month. She also reports she has missed work several times in the past 3 months due to not being able to get out of bed. When she was a teen, she was diagnosed as ADD. Now she is an adult, what are your initial thoughts for a diagnosis?

    a.   Attention Deficit Disorder
    b.   Mood Disorder
    c.   Obsessive Compulsive Disorder
    d.   Bipolar Disorder

75. Based in the scenario above, your initial questions should include:

    a.   Medical conditions
    b.   Past psychiatric care
    c.   Legal issues
    d.   All of the above

76. You have a client that describes situations where he becomes suicidal and had the means to complete the act. She is currently discussing suicide in her session. What should you do as her clinician?

    a.   Attention Deficit Disorder
    b.   Mood Disorder
    c.   Obsessive Compulsive Disorder
    d.   Bipolar Disorder

77. In the session above, what is the first thing you should do is what?

    a.   Call a crisis center
    b.   Assess clients suicidal thoughts
    c.   Discuss a safety plan
    d.   A and B

78. You receive a request from a client to release records to the court. You have not been this client's counselor in over 10 years. What is the standard for record retention?

    a.   5 years
    b.   10 years
    c.   15 years
    d.   Forever

79. Your client is involved in a court case. Your client asks that you speak to the probation officer and his lawyer. Under HIPAA, should you talk to them?

    a.   No, only with a subpoena.
    b.   Yes, If you receive written consent form your client with specified items that can be sent or discussed.
    c.   Yes, if the client requests communication, it is considered a consent.
    d.   No, only if client is in crisis

80. You get a call from a school social worker regarding a 10 year old client they would like to refer to you. The social worker states she does not have consent to discuss with you, but would like to give you information to see if you will take the case. What should you do?

    a.   Get information with all the details to make an informed decision
    b.   Get information but ask social worker not to tell you the name of the client
    c.   Discuss a safety plan
    d.   Ask the social worker to obtain a release and then call you to discuss.

81. Which therapy is associated with the exposure to a situation or stimulus while also experiencing some form of physical or emotional discomfort?

    a. Reinforcement training
    b. extinction therapy
    c. conditioning
    d. aversion therapy

82. Your neighbor and friend, reports that her 18 year old son is having legal issues. She reports also that she believes he is depressed. She asks you if you would be able to see him in your practice. How should you respond?

    a. Tell her you will see him, but only a few times to see if he is ok
    b. Refer him to someone in your practice
    c. Let her know that it is a conflict of interest and that you can give her a referral
    d. Take the case since you already have a rapport

83. You have been working with an adult client of the opposite sex. You have developed a good rapport, but you have noticed subtle hints of flirting in the past few sessions. Today your client asked if he could take you out for a coffee. What would be the best response?

    a.   Tell him you would love to and schedule a time.
    b.   Tell him you would love to, but it is against ethical regulations.
    c.   Explain that ethical regulations prevent intimate relationships with clients.
    d.   State that you have a working therapeutic relationship. It is important to keep boundaries. In addition, it is an   ethical violation. Then return back to the issues needing to be addressed in the session.

84. Which words are associated with the term "independent variable"?

    a. Response variable
    b. Predictor variable
    c. coefficients
    d. all of the above

85. What is the definition of the mean?

    a. The middle value in a range of values arranged in sequence by size

    b. The mean or average is the sum of all the numbers divided by the total amount of numbers

    c. The middle value divided by the total amount of numbers

    d. none of the above

86. What is the definition of the median?

    a. The middle value in a range of values arranged in sequence by size

    b. The mean or average is the sum of all the numbers divided by the total amount of numbers

    c. The middle value divided by the total amount of numbers

    d. none of the above

87. What is the definition of mode?

    a. The middle value in a range of values arranged in sequence by size

    b. The mean or average is the sum of all the numbers divided by the total amount of numbers

    c. The middle value divided by the total amount of numbers

    d. The most frequent number

88. What is a range?

    a. The lower limits of a range of scores

    b. The upper limits of a range of scores

    c. The upper and lower limits of a set of scores

    d. none of the above

89. Erik Erikson developed psychosocial stages of development. Which stage is a 1 ½ to 3 year old experiencing?

    a. Autonomy vs shame
    b. Initiative vs guilt
    c. Generativity vs stagnation
    d. Identity vs role confusion

90. Erik Erikson developed psychosocial stages of development. Which stage is a 1 ½ to 3 year old experiencing?

    a. Autonomy vs shame
    b. Industry vs inferiority
    c. Generativity vs stagnation
    d. Identity vs role confusion

91. Piaget developed the theory of cognitive stages of development. What stage are you in if you are able to think about the future and have abstract thinking?

    a. Sensorimotor
    b. Preoperational
    c. Operational
    d. Formal Operational

92. Freud believed that children at age3 3 were in what stage of development?

    a. Oral
    b. Anal
    c. Phallic
    d. Latency

93. According to Freud, what is called when you are stuck in a phase?

    a. Fixation
    b. Regression
    c. Stagnation
    d. Dualism

94. Leon Festinger developed a theory to evaluate behaviors by comparing a person's behaviors to others. What is this theory called?
   a. Social compromising theory
   b. Social comparison theory
   c. Socail stagnation theory
   d. none of the above

95. Carl Jung's analytical theory or achetypes described "persona". What is the definition?
   a. the archetype that represents our unconscious and conscious
   b. the archetype that represents our sex and life instincts
   c. the archetype that represents how we present ourselves to the world
   d. all of the above

96. Which theorist is noted with the term "behaviorism"?
   a.   Kohlberg
   b.   Erickson
   c.   Watson
   d.   Skinner

97. Which theorist is associated with REBT therapy?
   a.   Adler
   b.   Ellis
   c.   Freud
   d.   Erickson

98. REBT believes that you need to change _____ to change your behavior
   a.   Thinking
   b.   Feeling
   c.   Behavior
   d.   Health

99. What does the C in ABCDE model represent?

      a.   Continuum

      b.   Consequence

      c.   Conscious

      d.   Consciousness

100.   Aaron Beck is best associated with what theory?

      a.   Behavioral theory

      b.   Cognitive Behavioral Theory

      c.   Cognitive Theory

      d.   Psychosocial theory

Practice Test Answer Key

1. A	39. B
2. B	40. D
3. C	41. A
4. A	42. A
5. B	43. D
6. B	44. C
7. B	45. D
8. A	46. C
9. C	47. D
10. D	48. B
11. A	49. A
12. C	50. A
13. D	51. B
14. B	52. C
15. B	53. D
16. A	54. B
17. C	55. C
18. A	56. A
19. B	57. D
20. D	58. B
21. B	59. D
22. A	60. C
23. C	61. A
24. D	62. C
25. A	63. A
26. A	64. D
27. B	65. D
28. D	66. A
29. A	67. C
30. D	68. B
31. C	69. A
32. A	70. D
33. D	71. D
34. A	72. A
35. C	73. B
36. B	74. D
37. B	75. D
38. A	76. D

77. A	89. A
78. A	90. B
79. B	91. D
80. D	92. B
81. D	93. A
82. C	94. B
83. D	95. C
84. D	96. C
85. B	97. B
86. A	98. A
87. D	99. B
88. C	100. C

Exclusive Trivium Test Prep Test Tips and Study Strategies

Here at Trivium Test Prep, we strive to offer you the exemplary test tools that help you pass your exam the first time. This book includes an overview of important concepts, example questions throughout the text, and practice test questions. But we know that learning how to successfully take a test can be just as important as learning the content being tested. In addition to excelling on the NCE and CPCE Exam we want to give you the solutions you need to be successful every time you take a test. Our study strategies, preparation pointers, and test tips will help you succeed as you take the NCE and CPCE Exam and any test in the future!

Study Strategies

1. Spread out your studying. By taking the time to study a little bit every day, you strengthen your understanding of the testing material, so it's easier to recall that information on the day of the test. Our study guides make this easy by breaking up the concepts into sections with example practice questions, so you can test your knowledge as you read.

2. Create a study calendar. The sections of our book make it easy to review and practice with example questions on a schedule. Decide to read a specific number of pages or complete a number of practice questions every day. Breaking up all of the information in this way can make studying less overwhelming and more manageable.

3. Set measurable goals and motivational rewards. Follow your study calendar and reward yourself for completing reading, example questions, and practice problems and tests. You could take yourself out after a productive week of studying or watch a favorite show after reading a chapter. Treating yourself to rewards is a great way to stay motivated.

4. Use your current knowledge to understand new, unfamiliar concepts. When you learn something new, think about how it relates to something you know really well. Making connections between new ideas and your existing understanding can simplify the learning process and make the new information easier to remember.

5. Make learning interesting! If one aspect of a topic is interesting to you, it can make an entire concept easier to remember. Stay engaged and think about how concepts covered on the exam can affect the things you're interested in. The sidebars throughout the text offer additional information that could make ideas easier to recall.

6. Find a study environment that works for you. For some people, absolute silence in a library results in the most effective study session, while others need the background noise of a coffee shop to fuel productive studying. There are many websites that

generate white noise and recreate the sounds of different environments for studying. Figure out what distracts you and what engages you and plan accordingly.

7. Take practice tests in an environment that reflects the exam setting. While it's important to be as comfortable as possible when you study, practicing taking the test exactly as you'll take it on test day will make you more prepared for the actual exam. If your test starts on a Saturday morning, take your practice test on a Saturday morning. If you have access, try to find an empty classroom that has desks like the desks at testing center. The more closely you can mimic the testing center, the more prepared you'll feel on test day.

8. Study hard for the test in the days before the exam, but take it easy the night before and do something relaxing rather than studying and cramming. This will help decrease anxiety, allow you to get a better night's sleep, and be more mentally fresh during the big exam. Watch a light-hearted movie, read a favorite book, or take a walk, for example.

Preparation Pointers

1. Preparation is key! Don't wait until the day of your exam to gather your pencils, calculator, identification materials, or admission tickets. Check the requirements of the exam as soon as possible. Some tests require materials that may take more time to obtain, such as a passport-style photo, so be sure that you have plenty of time to collect everything. The night before the exam, lay out everything you'll need, so it's all ready to go on test day! We recommend at least two forms of ID, your admission ticket or confirmation, pencils, a high protein, compact snack, bottled water, and any necessary medications. Some testing centers will require you to put all of your supplies in a clear plastic bag. If you're prepared, you will be less stressed the morning of, and less likely to forget anything important.

2. If you're taking a pencil-and-paper exam, test your erasers on paper. Some erasers leave big, dark stains on paper instead of rubbing out pencil marks. Make sure your erasers work for you and the pencils you plan to use.

3. Make sure you give yourself your usual amount of sleep, preferably at least 7 – 8 hours. You may find you need even more sleep. Pay attention to how much you sleep in the days before the exam, and how many hours it takes for you to feel refreshed. This will allow you to be as sharp as possible during the test and make fewer simple mistakes.

4. Make sure to make transportation arrangements ahead of time, and have a backup plan in case your ride falls through. You don't want to be stressing about how you're going to get to the testing center the morning of the exam.

5. Many testing locations keep their air conditioners on high. You want to remember to bring a sweater or jacket in case the test center is too cold, as you never know how hot or cold the testing location could be. Remember, while you can always adjust for heat by removing layers, if you're cold, you're cold.

Test Tips

1. Go with your gut when choosing an answer. Statistically, the answer that comes to mind first is often the right one. This is assuming you studied the material, of course, which we hope you have done if you've read through one of our books!

2. For true or false questions: if you genuinely don't know the answer, mark it true. In most tests, there are typically more true answers than false answers.

3. For multiple-choice questions, read ALL the answer choices before marking an answer, even if you think you know the answer when you come across it. You may find your original "right" answer isn't necessarily the best option.

4. Look for key words: in multiple choice exams, particularly those that require you to read through a text, the questions typically contain key words. These key words can help the test taker choose the correct answer or confuse you if you don't recognize them. Common keywords are: *most*, *during*, *after*, *initially*, and *first*. Be sure you identify them before you read the available answers. Identifying the key words makes a huge difference in your chances of passing the test.

5. Narrow answers down by using the process of elimination: after you understand the question, read each answer. If you don't know the answer right away, use the process of elimination to narrow down the answer choices. It is easy to identify at least one answer that isn't correct. Continue to narrow down the choices before choosing the answer you believe best fits the question. By following this process, you increase your chances of selecting the correct answer.

6. Don't worry if others finish before or after you. Go at your own pace, and focus on the test in front of you.

7. Relax. With our help, we know you'll be ready to conquer the NCE and CPCE. You've studied and worked hard!

Keep in mind that every individual takes tests differently, so strategies that might work for you may not work for someone else. You know yourself best and are the best person to determine which of these tips and strategies will benefit your studying and test taking. Best of luck as you study, test, and work toward your future!

Made in the USA
Las Vegas, NV
08 April 2021

21006088R00070